MW00529491

BARACK OBAMA

INVISIBLE MAN

First published in 2017
by Eyewear Publishing Ltd
Suite 333, 19-21 Crawford Street
London, W1H 1PJ
United Kingdom

Graphic design by Edwin Smet
Cover photograph by Brooks Kraft
Author photograph by Sarah Masciotra
Printed in England by TJ International Ltd, Padstow, Cornwall

The editor has generally followed American spelling
and punctuation at the author's request.

Eyewear wishes to thank Jonathan Wonham
for his generous patronage of our press.

Set in Bembo 12 / 15 pt
ISBN 978-1-911335-30-6

WWW.EYEWEARPUBLISHING.COM

BARACK OBAMA

INVISIBLE MAN

DAVID MASCIOTRA

EYEWEAR PUBLISHING

Isaac Malcolm and Asha Kumasi, Russell

I hope you enjoy the book

love & happiness to you!

With love and gratitude
for my great teacher and true friend,
Roger Sullivan.

THE MIXTURE OF THE MARVELOUS
AND THE TERRIBLE IS A BASIC CONDITION
OF HUMAN LIFE, AND THE PERSISTENCE
OF HUMAN IDEALS REPRESENTS THE
MARVELOUS PULLING ITSELF UP OUT
OF THE CHAOS OF THE UNIVERSE.

RALPH ELLISON

THE INVISIBLE MAN

Barack Obama was the invisible president. He was invisible simply because people refused to see him. Just as Ralph Ellison's unnamed narrator explained about his curious existence of permanent placement in the optical shadows, paranoiacs see him as a 'figure in a nightmare which the sleeper tries with all his strength to destroy.' Meanwhile, the mind best at dilution, and absent the intellectual equipment to deal with the complexity of humanity, reduces Obama to a symbol. He becomes a statue, but unlike a stone construction with a face locked into hospitable expression, he has the capability to challenge the onlooker and uplift the observer, just as he has the potential to disappoint the viewer.

The protagonist of *Invisible Man* diagnoses those whose minds erase his human features and characteristics as suffering from a 'peculiar disposition of the eyes' – the 'inner eyes with which they look through their physical eyes upon reality.' Psychologists would call the inner eyes 'consciousness.' An individuated consciousness frames the focus of all experience, and instructs and guides, sometimes with the inscrutable properties of the best mystery, the individual how to receive and perceive everything. The election of Barack Obama – a black man with an Arabic-rooted name after slavery and segregation, and at the height of cultural anxiety over Islam – collided with the consciousness of many Americans. Among the wreckage and in the casualty count, was the vision of the American public, and the capacity to rationally observe, absorb, and interpret the president.

The beautiful and brutal story of American development, always in progress and often moving backward, differs from the Shakespearean statement of existential despair. It is not, as Macbeth understood life, 'a tale told by an idiot, full of sound and fury, signifying nothing.' The linearity of American history is traceable only according to the expansion of freedom and the enlargement of liberty. In 1776, only white men who owned property could vote, the indigenous wore a target for expulsion and exploitation, and men who looked like Barack Obama qualified only for chains. Before Americans can pop champagne bottles in a celebration of themselves, they must realize that every inch of conquest for liberty and justice required a bitter and bloody war of collision. Whenever a group of Americans – black, gay, female – demand inclusion in the American experiment of self-governance, they face violent and vicious opposition. The struggle of American history pitting the outsider, the underdog, the underclass against the powerful, wealthy, and often elected is the tale told, not by an idiot, but often to idiots – idiots who make themselves ignorant with their refusal to open their eyes and see. The blindfold over the inner eyes is much too thick for the outer eyes to function properly.

For millions of voluntarily blind Americans, the act of witnessing Barack Obama deliver his victory speech on November 4, 2008, shortly after the concession of an elderly, white war hero, caused post-traumatic stress disorder. They could no longer function as adults with clear eyes and clear thoughts. They would spend the next eight years speaking and acting as if they were habitual users of hallucinatory drugs – seeing the ominous signs of conspiracy, destruction, and subversion in every wink, grin, and gesture of the alien occupying the Oval Office. They believed and propagated the idea that Obama was an agent acting to undermine America, and in some ways – but not how they thought – they were correct. Regardless of policy, and his policies were not outside the mainstream, Obama undermined the mythic America of perfection – the 'shining city on the hill' that Ronald Reagan, America's greatest contemporary mythmaker, boasted of – by framing focus on reality; a reality that, despite its tragic and traumatic dimensions, maintains greater beauty and inspiration than the myth. Barack Obama's election was only unprecedented, and for many, unpredictable, because of America's history of bigotry and oppression. To the Americans who tacitly approve of oppression, or choose to act as if it does not exist, Obama's victory sent a signal: Your story is not relevant. Your fantasy is no longer a believable story. It is not that America is or is not great, but that America must always strive to become great. The election of a black man, who would not have been able to vote just decades earlier, to the presidency is a significant hammer in the nail in the construction of greatness.

Many other Americans, while not as deranged and demented as those who saw in Obama a monstrous force of evil and subversion, diminished Obama as person, dispossessed him as president, and deracinated him into symbol. Because his mere victory was a revolutionary act of symbolic transformation at the height of American power, many voters believed that his presidency would possess revolutionary potential of equal power. Any imperfection in policy or rhetoric from President Obama would undermine this unrealistic faith claim, and expose him, in the debilitated inner eyes, as a fraud. To the sympathetic, but delusional, white liberal, Obama was not a normal human being. He was a blank screen waiting for them to project their fondest fantasies and deepest wishes. Any blemish on that screen would result in its destruction. Fallibility is intolerable to those searching for a messiah. Unrealistic expectations, due to an overinvestment in Obama's symbolic power, created conditions conducive to the eventual erasure of Obama's identity and achievements. A statue does not speak. So, it certainly will not utter words unfriendly to the desires of the onlooker. A statue does not move. It cannot walk in a direction unfamiliar to the observer.

Simultaneous with the reduction of Obama into symbol was the refusal of many voters and critics to acknowledge the value of symbol, and the power of the symbolic alteration of the American image Obama authored. What would it mean for black children to have their formative experiences as citizens with a black man as national leader, chief executive, and commander? What would it mean for white children? What would it mean for the Muslim and non-Muslim immigrants and natural born Americans who had names like Barack and Hussein? What would it mean for all of the adults in interracial marriages, and more consequentially, the children conceived within those unions?

These important questions hung in the air like a thick fog on a city street. Americans, risking an emotional crash, drove through with abandon, foot on the gas and hands steady on the steering wheel. White America had grown so accustomed to, and physically and spiritually invested in, white leadership of American institutions that it could not fully grasp the black hue of the White House. Obama shattered the ultimate glass ceiling, and among the shards of glass, were the broken fragments of white illusion. White superiority, and perhaps more importantly, white authority could no longer be taken for granted. While symbolism is insufficient for the task of political improvement, it is through symbol that human beings develop an understanding of their own stories. When Obama took the oath of office, he shattered a symbol that, for many white Americans, was essential to their story, and replaced it with something from an area of American history previously kept undercover. That high level act has a low level application. It moves from pathos to the pavement.

When I developed into adolescence and then early adulthood, it seemed entirely natural that the president, along with the mayor and the governor, always looked like my father, or my uncle, or like a much older version of myself. Michele Wallace, a black writer and professor, recalls the opposite experience as a school child in 1960s New York. She writes that she can 'still remember the stricken look' on her teacher's face when she announced that she wanted to become president when she grew up. For much of its history, the subtext of the adjective, 'American,' was 'white.' White is normal and universal, while other races and ethnicities require their own special days on the calendar, television networks, subgenres of literature, and university departments. Obama's ascension to the mountaintop of imperial and cultural command demolished all the natural assumptions of the American order. On night one, Obama's impact created too large of a crater in the collective consciousness of the citizenry for him to enjoy a normal presidency. The right wing, in their distortion of him into a monster, set him up to fail, but so did the left wing, in their hopes of him as a messiah. The moderates in the middle often seemed disconnected from the essence and existence of Obama, having arguments about the man they treated as a pedestrian on a crosswalk during an afternoon stroll.

An interesting and revealing criticism of President Obama grew increasingly popular among conservative commentators at around the midway point of the presidency. *National Review*, *Fox News*, and other familiar sources of right wing reportage began to brand and bash Obama as 'lazy' and 'absentee' for his reportedly 'unprecedented' and 'excessive' vacation and golf getaways. Those same outlets soon issued a similar indictment of Obama's 'refusal' to host press conferences. Eventually, the mainstream media channeled the same story through their own, much louder amplifier, and the idea of Obama as a reclusive president has shaped public perception of his performance, with many Americans often commenting how they 'never saw him.' [1]

It turns out that Obama had taken fewer vacation days than any president since Jimmy Carter, and that he averaged two press conferences a month – more than Reagan, Carter, Ford and Nixon, the same as Clinton, and slightly less than both George H.W. Bush and George W. Bush.

The attack on Obama's absenteeism read like much more than mere partisan insult. In addition to playing on old stereotypes against black men, it also demonstrated the blindness of those who say it and believe it. They actually could not see Barack Obama. He was in the White House – not on vacation – and he was speaking to the press, but millions of Americans believed otherwise. They do not see him, because they cannot see him. They see only what their imaginations allow them to see, and from the vantage point of that odd and obstructed view, a postmodern mystery of politics emerges to haunt America in the 21st century: Does President Barack Obama exist?

Is the former President – not the monster, messiah, or statue – real? If so, who is he? What has he accomplished? What are his failures? What is his influence? How does he operate as symbol, and what is the substance of the man?

Karl Marx famously commented that 'history repeats itself first as tragedy, then as farce.' The tragic and farcical are present side by side, at the same time, in the current American condition. When Barack Obama entered office in 2008, the country was in financial free fall due to reckless, negligent, and possibly criminal, behavior on the part of its most powerful economic institutions. Bipartisan governmental policy colluded with corporate malfeasance to create the catastrophe of home foreclosures, mortgage lender collapse, and the liquidation of middle class wealth. Unemployment rates were rising with the rapidity of a rocket, and many respectable and credible analysts were calling out a code red; ringing all alarms in their prediction of another Great Depression. At the end of Obama's term, unemployment was at near historic lows, the housing market had recovered, and the stock market had doubled its immediate post-crash level.

When the president signed his groundbreaking and history-making health care reform bill into law, pundits took on the solemn mood and grave demeanor of a doctor preparing to tell a family he lost their loved one on the surgical table. They warned that the new law would force hospitals to ration care and deprive the elderly of treatment. They appeared hysterical as they speculated that health care costs would become punitive and prohibitive. Eventually, patients of all kinds would enter a state of physical misery unknown to inhabitants of the wealthy, Western world. Meanwhile, new regulations requiring large employers to offer all full time workers health care coverage would set up incentives for a 'part time economy' in which people could, at best, attain only marginal attachment to the labor force. Audible in none of the shrieks of terror was the acknowledgement that America's privatized, for-profit system of health care already rationed medicine according to wealth. It already attached exorbitant price tags to standard treatment, and it already exerted an injurious pull on the relationship between labor and management. The invisibility of Obama, once he declared his intention to reform health care administration and law, erased the long term and short-term memory of many Americans, causing America to also become invisible. Polling data demonstrates that prior to the passage of the Affordable Care Act, eight out of ten Americans supported a significant overhaul of the health insurance system, and that over sixty percent approved of government intervention to guarantee universal coverage. Obama maneuvered to achieve just those aims, and suddenly millions of Americans acted as if the, often tragic and horrific, health care system of their country was without flaw.[2]

The apocalyptic ravings of Republicans, media commentators, and political forecasters were as wrong on health care as they were on economic conditions. Because of the passage of the Affordable Care Act into law, twenty million people now have health care coverage who had previously lacked it, insurance premiums are increasing at the slowest and lowest rates on record, and the medical debt of Americans is also at its lowest point.[3] The tragedy is that Barack Obama, despite significant flaws and failures, has a record of accomplishment few modern presidents could claim, but neither political wing is able to acknowledge it. The right wing, because of its derangement and for the sake of its own acumen, must act as if Obama is a combination of Vladimir Lenin and Herbert Hoover – obliviously incompetent and diabolically efficient at the same time. While the left should defend the progress made possible by liberal reform, and advocate for more of it, it too is busy acting as if America has descended into a circle of Hell not even Dante could imagine. Despite having one of the highest standards of living in the history of the world, Americans increasingly tell polling data firms that everything is in decline and a disaster.[4] There is a deficit of avidity that inflicts greater harm upon the country than any fiscal imbalance. The deficit results from strain on the national spirit from both left and right. One of Obama's cultural missions was to combat the strain, and inject an antidote of hope into the body politic, but, struggling against his own invisibility, such an ambitious project of consciousness creativity proved out of reach.

The extremes of American political discourse, which due to social media control more of the conversational territory, are so committed to their conflicting, but oddly complementary, narratives of destruction that they both vaporize Obama's achievements, and cause Obama himself to vanish. The farce is that while depictions of Obama, and the country over which he presided, continue to become more dramatic and panicked, the former president continues to become more mild mannered and moderate. It is a comedy of gallows humor, but as the disastrous nomination and horrific victory of Donald Trump demonstrates, the consequences are not a laughing matter. The entire candidacy of Donald Trump was partially the result of the viral spread of the idea that America is a country in free fall and irreversible decline. 'Broken,' 'rigged,' and 'corrupt' are the key adjectives commentators and constituents, of left and right, use to describe the United States. The demagogue delights in hysteria, because without it, demagoguery is ineffective. All of the arcane and esoteric analysis of Trump's alarming rise to the presidency seeks to avoid the most truthful, but also painful, conclusion: The American people invited and chauffeured him there. Barack Obama's invisible status was crucial to the catastrophic invitation. If the right wing did not believe that Obama was Lucifer's apprentice, they would have nominated a normal, sane Republican to wrestle the White House out of Democratic control, just as they did in 2012. Two thirds of Trump voters, according to surveys, believed that the election of 2016 was 'America's last chance.'[5] When Trump, in perfection of the demagogue's dialect, announced that the country was broken, and 'I alone can fix it,' most Republicans agreed. If the left did not mistake Obama for a corporate sycophant without any real principles, they could have more effectively challenged the conservative narrative of the American apocalypse, and they would not have shown such resistance to the candidacy of Obama's Secretary of State, Hillary Clinton. Eight years of historical amnesia, political blindness, and racial hallucination made the Trump nomination and victory possible. As disastrous as it seems, it served an important, albeit destructive, purpose in American life.

Barack Obama's invisibility is vital to the fragile psyches of both left and right. Committed to a monolithic America that never existed outside of racist law and convention, and motivated by a nostalgia for an America that had not yet evolved into America, the right wing must oppose Obama, and present him as a pariah, because he is not only the representation of a new America, he is its culmination. Demographic shifts in the nation indicate that in the near future, white people will constitute a minority. Black and brown Americans are gaining authority and influence in political, economic, cultural, and educational institutions, while the arrival of immigrants continues to enhance the multiplicity of faces that construct the American identity. White people are now a minority in 78 American counties. New York, Washington D.C., Las Vegas, Memphis, and several other formerly white cities now have 'majority-minority' populations.[6] Contrary to the fantasy of many nostalgic whites, racial and ethnic minorities are not parasites fit for deportation or desperate for white rescue. The most educated groups of Americans, respectively, are Nigerian immigrants and black women.[7] Many whites, especially conservative whites uncomfortable with change and liberal growth, feel as if they are hanging on to a fraying rope for dear life. To realize and recognize that Obama was an impressive and inspired administrator, communicator, and leader is to welcome an anxiety attack of great severity. Obama himself, in a characteristic moment of insightful observation, once wondered aloud if, given the demographic changes that are inevitable but still not final, he came along twenty years too early. The immediate consequence of his early arrival was the election of Donald Trump, who, for all of his surreal success, represents the last gasp of the white conservative. The panic of that realization overwhelmed the faculties of many white voters, and in their intellectually debilitated state, voted for a conman who bragged about committing sexual assault, and revealed himself to have no knowledge of constitutional law, civics, or politics.

Meanwhile, much of the left must act as if Obama is a 'poster child for the death of the liberal class,' as grim reaper Chris Hedges put it, or that his accomplishments are insignificant, in the adoption of an anti-intellectual position resistant to any sophisticated understanding of the challenges of triumvirate government, because to appreciate the more nuanced and truthful account of events would undermine their demand for 'political revolution.' [8] It would also rob them of the glamour that accompanies the ideological purity of the protest movement.

However historians evaluate Obama's legacy, the most politically active, white constituents of both parties have seemed to form an unspoken agreement that he cannot become another Jackie Robinson. Robinson broke the color barrier of professional baseball, but he did so with undeniable excellence. The burden on his shoulders was the equivalent of a hundred pound stone, because he was swinging bats and stealing bases for the entire race. If he failed, no one knows how long it would have taken for the MLB to sign another black player. His success meant that white general managers, white journalists, and white fans had no choice but to acknowledge the existence of black talent. Such existence demands placement at the highest levels of play. If Obama is a great president, or even a good president, which is significant because many presidents, like his predecessor, were awful, corrupt, or some combination of both, he presents a challenge beyond symbol to the entirety of the white establishment. The accomplishment of Barack Obama might shine an unflattering light on the absence of black governors throughout the United States, the rarity of black mayors in major cities, and the relatively small number of blacks in the House and Senate. In *Dreams from My Father*, Obama writes about, shortly after his arrival in Chicago to work as a community organizer, hearing many black men in barbershops and black women in living rooms discuss the importance of the election of Harold Washington as Chicago's first black mayor. Black residents of Chicago, including those who never believed such a political victory was possible, straightened their backs and held their heads high. Their ambitions were suddenly made larger, and their encouragement for their children, suddenly stronger.

It is difficult for anyone lucid to argue that Obama has not had the same effect, but his success, and the widespread celebration of his success, would magnify and multiply that effect. It would also give a forceful answer to the intractable question, what is an American?

Walt Whitman wrote that America was a new nation in need of new poets. *Leaves of Grass* was not only a masterful poem, but also his nomination of a 'new Bible' for the unique and unprecedented citizen of a unique and unprecedented nation. America, like the poet himself, contradicts itself, and contains multitudes. Whitman writes that he 'speaks the password primeval' and gives the 'sign of democracy,' both of which include the voices of slaves, prostitutes, the diseased and the despairing, and of thieves and dwarves. He feels at home in the fleet of iceboats, on the hills of Vermont, in the woods of Maine, and on a Texan ranch. The great poet envisioned an 'out of many, one' nation, where, like a field of 'hopeful green stuff,' each leaf is individual and distinct, but has communion with the rest. The grass itself then becomes sacramental to Whitman. It is a 'uniform hieroglyphic' and the 'uncut hair of graves,' growing 'among black folks as among white, Kanuck, Tuckahoe, Congressman, and Cuff.' The personality and personhood of American character and citizenship requires ambition as large as Whitman's imagination. Obama is a line out of Whitman's poem, but it is an epic poem of pain, as much as it is a secular prayer for renewal. The distance between the American imagination and the American experience is too often measurable with lines of corpses, and in instruments of disappointment. As the distance closes – and the American identity undergoes yet another metamorphosis – tears of joy and terror water the soil underneath the grass. The ground in Grant Park, where Obama gave his first presidential victory speech, was certainly wet that night, and remains so years later. In 2016, tears of a different emotion soaked many streets throughout the country, and around the world, as America revealed an ugly face; rejecting the nation of Whitman's poetry and the constitution's promise to welcome back the country of exclusion, threat, and mediocrity.

The identity of the average American is elusive, and shrouded in mystery, because America is the first nation, and Whitman was the first to capture it, that made unity possible through individuality and diversity. As America continues to become much more multicultural and diverse since the initial publication of *Leaves of Grass* in 1855, Barack Obama is an avatar for its multiethnic and multicultural character. Born in Hawaii, to a white woman from Kansas and an African man from Kenya, he spent several years of his childhood in Indonesia, and studied in California and New York before eventually landing in Chicago. Black, white, with an Arabic name and an eclectic background, he contains multitudes, and contradicts himself. The United States of America has a 'representational' form of government. Citizens vote for a leader to not only represent their interests, but actually represent them – speak for them, grieve for them, celebrate for them, and advocate for them in local, national, and international disputes and developments.

Barack Obama, even for those who became apoplectic at the thought, represented all Americans, in domestic affairs and global activities, for eight years. That could cause a crisis of consciousness for anyone operating under the illusion that his ethnic and ancestral background makes him superior to his representative.

Any inquiry into the state of American identity – the mystery of what it means 'to be' American – will inevitably include complexity and contradiction. Taking for granted a white face of power leads to the assumption that whiteness is natural and normal in decision-making roles. Blackness then becomes unnatural and abnormal. During the years of Obama's tenure as president, it might have seemed natural and normal to black children to think of the president – the ultimate leader and decision-maker – as black. It might also strike the white child as curious that the president was not white. Such a radical transformation in the aesthetic of American power produces irrevocable changes in the collective psyche, regardless of presidential intention or public awareness. Filmmaker Steve McQueen confessed in a conversation with Cornel West that had Obama never entered the White House, he would not have gained the confidence to champion, and ultimately, direct the Academy Award-winning film, *12 Years a Slave*.[9] Cinematic depiction of black life and heroism followed with *The Butler, Selma, Hidden Figures, Moonlight*, and many other groundbreaking films.

Obama shifted the schematics of the cultural ground. Displays and pronouncements of black beauty and pride became normal in entertainment, while Black Lives Matter, due to many factors, grew into a legitimate force in local and national politics. Beyoncé, the nation's most popular singer, infused into her public and viral video performances displays of black love and resistance to white supremacy. Conservative critics cried with characteristic cowardice, but young Americans – white and black – did not seem to mind, at least, as far as record sales and concert attendance indicates. Similar polarization played out after several high profile black football players staged a silent protest of police brutality by taking a knee during the national anthem. Just as Harold Washington empowered black residents of Chicago, effectively handing them an amplifier of confidence to broadcast their concerns and convictions, Obama, by his presidential presence, elevated blackness to a pedestal of prominence in American life. The cumulative effect of emerging black pride and beauty in politics and pop culture is to reassure the child in the classroom, listening to her teacher, or the child in the living room, watching his television. Rather than receiving the message from a dominant white culture, 'everything will be okay, if you'll be like me,' the child, having inculcated encouragement from someone no less than the president, entertains the abridgment, 'everything will be okay.'

'Make America Great Again,' the imbecilic and historically illiterate slogan of the Trump campaign, as many commentators have pointed out, was a nostalgic call for time travel back to the era of uncontested white dominance. Multiple studies and surveys indicate that the majority of the American people do not pay close attention to political or economic developments. One credible poll found that nearly one third of Americans, during the Obama administration, could not name the vice president.[10] Analysts who believe people voted for Trump because of sophisticated arguments over twenty-five-year-old trade deals are delusional. Trump's election was an argument over culture. The invisible Barack Obama became a subversive agent against American tradition. Trump promises to nullify the Obama effect. At the same time, many white Americans observed the cultural influence of Obama, and pined for the days when blacks knew their role, and remained in geographic and metaphorical ghettos. A *Washington Post* poll found that over half of Trump voters believe that 'diversity comes at the expense of whites.' [11] In a sense, they are correct, because they do not mean at the expense of white freedom, happiness, or opportunity. They mean white power. Every time Obama performed his ceremonial role as nation's representative, or the Academy Awards honored a black filmmaker, or Beyoncé donned a sultry costume in Black Panther style, too many whites – the same whites who would celebrate Trump – thought, 'this is happening at our expense.'

The presidential personality creates a chain reaction of cultural reform, irrespective of public policy. John F. Kennedy, with his glamour, wit, and sensual appeal, preceded the sexual revolution, in stark contrast to the sterile and dull Dwight D. Eisenhower, who seemed to typify the zipped up, middle class morality of the 1950s. Reagan resuscitated one-note nationalism for a public unwilling to do the heavy lifting of introspection, and undergo the self-criticism necessary for the diagnostic work of dealing with the disease at the heart of its narcissistic culture. President Carter, Reagan's predecessor, attempted to initiate the process of maturation, but failed in what amounts to a small tragedy. Reagan, for better and certainly for worse, had a much more effectual cultural personality.

If one returns to the elementary school, it becomes clear that the children learning to read and write are set to inherit an America far different than the country familiar to baby boomers, and elderly citizens – a country far different from the one Reagan so effortlessly understood and manipulated. When I dated a black girl in high school, interracial coupling still carried the whiff of danger and rebellion. Both an aphrodisiac and an insult, we were made to feel as if our behavior was outside the mainstream. When the President of the United States is the product of an interracial marriage, it is impossible for anything to become more mainstream than a biracial ancestral background. For too long, American law, politics, and pop culture undermined Whitman's promise and prognosis of integration. The definition of America is never static, as it continually evolves, develops, regresses, and progresses. Barack Obama's ascendancy as American spokesperson, executive, and representative in an increasingly interconnected and globalized world constitutes a major adaptation of America in the survival of its soul. Obama is many things at once, but he is indisputably, American.

It is for precisely the reason of Obama's reorientation of American identity that before he won election, an absurd conspiracy theory emerged to question his legitimacy. The 'birther' movement posits that Obama, due to some psychic foresight and political ambition of his American mother, was actually born in Kenya, but his parents made it appear as if he was born in Hawaii. A contemporaneous announcement of his birth in a small, Hawaiian newspaper, along with the eventual publication of his birth certificate, did little to penetrate the iron skulls of birther believers. It is an error for optimists to dismiss the birther conspiracy as the lunatic property of fringe territory. According to credible studies and surveys, 51 percent of registered Republicans believe that Barack Obama was 'probably born in another country,' and 61 percent of Donald Trump primary voters were confident that the then-president of the United States was actually an illegal immigrant.[12] Trump's entire introduction to Republican politics was as unofficial spokesman of the movement to discredit the authenticity of Obama's American citizenship. At one point, Trump even claimed to have hired a team of investigators who were making 'unbelievable, incredible' discoveries in Hawaii.[13] It was a smarmy but savvy move for Trump to use his celebrity to amplify the birther theory, because at that point, no legitimate Republican would touch it, much less endorse it. Trump ingratiated himself to millions of committed Republican voters by giving credibility to their paranoid fantasies. While other Republicans refused to comment or rejected birtherism altogether, the ignorant base gravitated toward the only man who, in their view, rose above political correctness to speak the real truth. Birthers constitute a majority of the Republican votership, and an overwhelming majority of the support for Trump. The popularity of a conspiracy theory so fundamentally and visibly absurd boasts the potency of the hallucinogenic drug that is white anxiety.

The birther conspiracy is easy for many people to take seriously, not because it rises to even a minimal level of coherence, but because it provides intellectual cover for the visceral, borderline primal, and undoubtedly tribal, hatred of Obama. Obama as culmination of America's expansion of hospitality and authority to racial and ethnic minorities, and the erosion of white only territory, is not real, if he is not really an American. Because most of the American right refuses to see Obama as a 'real American,' the birther conspiracy theory satiates their emotional wound resulting from disappearance of cultural control.

In a perfect, and unintentional, demonstration of America's inability to see Obama, and their relegation of him into a role of invisibility, Clint Eastwood addressed the 2012 Republican Party Convention by having a pretend conversation with Barack Obama. An empty chair represented the sitting President. The truth is that those who applauded Eastwood's bizarre attempt at mockery always see an empty chair when they look at Obama. Then, they fill the chair with the image they have invented – the maniacal usurper of American ideals, the rabid Marxist, or the closeted Muslim fanatic who sympathizes with suicide bombers. Eastwood's biggest applause line of the night was his declaration that 'this is our country.' To witness, in 2012, a political party with an 89 percent white membership scream like children meeting Santa Claus when an elderly white movie star claims exclusive ownership of a country with a black president and a rapidly diversifying public, is to gain understanding of how racial resentment, and nostalgia for ethnic authority, drives the Republican Party, and much of its hysterical opposition to Obama.[14] Race as motivator for the American right became undeniable when Donald Trump was actually strengthened by what many media analysts predicted would undermine his campaigns – the castigation of Mexican immigrants as 'rapists' and 'bad people bringing drugs,' the advocacy of a prohibition on Muslim immigration, and the depiction of African American life as 'hell.'

Senator Bernie Sanders, and the left wing response to his failed campaign for the presidency, also showed signs of white voters diving to grab back white authority as if it were a wild pitch. First, Sanders dismissed Clinton's dominant victories in states where most Democratic primary voters are black as 'insignificant' wins in the 'conservative Deep South,' and the mass media amplified his white-centric vision of the electorate by constantly offering analysis of the 'enthusiasm gap' between Sanders and Clinton.[15] Clinton won over three million more votes than Sanders, garnering massive margins of victory with black and Latino voters, but narrowly losing among white Democrats in several states. Implementing standard journalistic standards of evaluation would give any rational observer the idea that excitement exists for a candidate only when he can claim victory of the white vote. The support of millions of black and Latino voters constitute an 'enthusiasm deficit' and 'crisis of confidence.' The hold on liberalism, like the claim to Americanism, wears a 'white only' sign. During Obama's first race for the presidency in 2008, when his opponent was also Hillary Clinton, former President Bill Clinton clumsily attempted to offer the same dismissal of nonwhite voters as defense of his candidate's eventual defeat. In South Carolina, when it was clear that Barack Obama, carried to victory by black voters, would dominate that state's primary, Clinton shrugged off Obama's success by saying, 'Jesse Jackson won in South Carolina twice, in 1984 and '88.' Even though Jackson's underrated campaigns were profoundly influential on American politics, and the Democratic Party in particular, the implication was clearly that blacks could win in South Carolina, because of black voters, but not achieve much else. The serious and safe candidate is the white one. Sanders and Clinton are too sophisticated to not realize the subtle racial signal they were flashing – a signal that whispers to whites, 'Do you want to associate with us whites, or go out there on the fringe with the blacks?'

As important as race remains to American culture, and as much as it persists as a political and psychological problem, the reasons that America tailored a cloak of invisibility for President Obama trespass far beyond the color line. For all of its vitality and variety, in many ways, the United States of America is a cultural disaster zone. Richard Hofstadter, in one of the most important books of 20th century American history, documented and described the 'anti-intellectual' streak that runs through America, while sociologist Barry Glassner, along with many others, has exposed the mass media, political class, and general public's collusion in the creation of a 'culture of fear.' The trauma of the terrorist attacks on September 11, 2001, followed closely by the financial crisis of 2008, only exacerbated the anxiety and despair of the average American. American pop culture went from a near parody of euphoria and hope to a dark funeral parlor full of nothing but rotting corpses and dry bones. Once-childish venues of entertainment, such as superhero movies, have become dark explorations of cynicism. Nothing dominates visual entertainment like visions of violence, while young adult literature and Hollywood blockbusters continue to tell tales of woe set in dystopian wastelands. Given that entertainment is escapism, one has to wonder if many Americans, unhappy with their lives, fantasize about the world blowing up. Donald Trump is both a verifier and vehicle for that fantasy.

The current president of the United States called America a 'hellhole,' and according to most studies and surveys, a large majority of Americans are despondent about their lives, and fearful of the future, convinced their children will have worse lives than they currently endure. Thirteen percent of Americans now take anti-depressant drugs.[16] Even a cursory look at news headlines presents a picture of the world inching toward Armageddon – ISIS will blow up the universe, climate change will reduce the planet to a ball of flaming gas, and due to rising rates of income inequality, everyone outside the one percent will soon snort and paw at the ground for bread crusts, before they crawl back to their alleyway homes. There is overwhelming data to prove that, in terms of life expectancy, general health, education, and standard of living, 2015 was the greatest year for the species on record, but most Americans are emotionally committed to a politicized narrative of destruction.[17] Catastrophes await around every corner, and the only aid and comfort in such an unending crisis, is to affix blame. Meanwhile, surveys indicate that, despite unprecedented access to educational institutions, Americans have little knowledge of history, geography, international affairs, and the natural sciences. Universities continue to conform to a corporate model of business training in curricula to appease a public that increasingly equates education with career preparation, and little else.

So, what happens when America's president is the most intellectual, calm, rational, and hopeful in modern history? Not since John F. Kennedy had an American leader attempted to inspire Americans to appreciate the blessings in their lives, and look beyond present predicaments into a luminescent future of faith and fortification. Obama's campaign slogans of 'Hope and Change' and 'Yes We Can' become oddly interesting, and possibly combative, in a culture invested in despair and death, while mentally chanting, 'No, we can't.' In 2008 and 2012, Obama won while describing America as a flawed, but fundamentally promising place where people, like him, can overcome the odds to construct and conduct lives of pleasure, achievement, and love. In 2016, Donald Trump won while denigrating America as a 'giant crime scene.' The only place in the country where so much had changed in merely eight years was the mind of the average voter.

President Obama, much to the chagrin and frustration of his more emotive left wing sympathizers, always attempted to elevate the public discourse by conducting himself with quiet elegance, dignity, and grace. While Americans fought over the frivolous with intense hostility on social media, Obama refused to insult or mock his opponents. In an era when Americans have trouble expressing themselves with eloquence, continually debasing the English language, Obama maintains a rhetorical style blending the professorial and poetic. In an age of anxiety and climate of cynicism in which right wing commentators glibly announce that 'America is finished' and left wing activists claim that 'democracy is dead,' Obama celebrates the state of the country, and asks for faith in future achievements, enhancements of justice, and elevation of personal happiness. For all of the imbecilic and racist condemnation of Obama as 'un-American,' he does fly in the face of the cultural flow. He does not display or indulge the contemporary American passion for panic and pessimism. Americans had an optic challenge with their president, because he speaks in a language many of them cannot understand and appreciate, and he carries himself with an ease that eludes them, as they are too weighed down with worry and too intoxicated by 'if it bleeds, it leads' television coverage, to settle into a peaceful state of mind. Trump, in the meantime, speaks at a middle school reading level, according to linguistic studies, and boasts of his own vulgarity.

Many Americans accuse Obama of having an aloof detachment to reality, or having a narcissistic personality, because he, from their obstructed viewpoint, does not sufficiently connect to the crises of American life. In reality, Obama – through his policy successes and failures – demonstrated the resolute leadership of Franklin Roosevelt, who famously announced in the death throes of the Great Depression and World War II, 'We have nothing to fear but fear itself.' To an increasingly agitated public, a calm leader will appear to have an offensive disconnectedness, and to an increasingly frightened public, a rational president will appear 'out of touch,' while a histrionic leader receives credit for 'tapping into' the public mood. Obama is a stoic, and to have seen him clearly might have offered hope and help to the observant citizen to regain composure in an unpredictable world, but the culture is too far over the edge of hysteria to grab hold of the helping hand of reality.

The cultural dynamics, national politics, and racial anxiety of the United States coalesced to form overwhelming odds against the visibility and persuasive success of its first African American president. A majority of voters freely elected Obama, not once but twice, but were not ready for the implications and consequences of his victory. Similar to an unhappy marriage, those within the union knew not how to speak or behave. Obama, as president, was one of the most visible men in the country, but Obama, as a person, remained invisible. This contradiction contains the tragedy of his presidency.

The protagonist of *Invisible Man* writes that the world moves 'not like an arrow, but a boomerang.' 'Beware of those who speak of the spiral of history,' he warns, 'They are preparing a boomerang. Keep a steel helmet handy.' The election of Barack Obama soared like a boomerang into the atmosphere of history, where Dr. King once promised that the winds always blow in the direction of justice, but not long after Obama's inauguration, he and his supporters started to suffer head wounds from the boomerang returning, and landing, just as hard – a sad preview of the concussive blow of Trump's electoral victory. The inability of the right, and left, to clearly see Obama inhibited the implementation of his agenda, at points, but one also has to wonder if he benefited from invisibility, just as Ellison's narrator reaps certain rewards. The 'invisible man' lives in a basement apartment in New York without paying rent. His race, and invisible status, allows him to go undetected as he enters and exits the building, and he is free to squat in the unused unit.

Ellison's protagonist, having secured housing without cost, has covered every inch of available wall space with light bulbs, and hung other light fixtures from the ceiling. When he sits alone in his room, his setting becomes the sun. It is a mystery if the extreme luminosity of the room – making it almost translucent – exists to illuminate him, like a spotlight. Is it how he would like to walk through an indifferent universe, so that it is impossible for pedestrians to overlook or ignore him? Or is the light so bright that it becomes blinding? Would any visitor experience something similar to looking directly into the eye of the sun? When inside his home, is he able to retreat back into a state of invisibility in order to avoid seeing himself?

In *Dreams from My Father*, Obama struggles to discover his true identity. He searches for the father he never knew, and attempts to excavate the African roots he never could plant. Part of his personality, character, and spirit – just like those properties within every human being – would forever remain just out of sight, like the smiling face of a woman wearing a veil. It is difficult to determine if she is smiling with love, or with the evil that comes from someone who knows something you don't, and is happy about it. As a result of his adversity, and in response to the debris he had to deflect from his face as he tried to look in the mirror and peer into the future, Obama developed into a political and philosophical pragmatist. He came to believe in that which is tangible and measurable. Theories and principles are no match for results, especially when the quality of people's lives is at stake.

Pragmatism is the philosophical methodology and political technique of a mature and sophisticated leader. It demands an awareness of reality, and an adherence to the limits of reality. Americans, simultaneously sorting through multiple traumas – 9/11, the financial crisis, white anxiety over loss of authority – cannot appreciate the pragmatist. The pragmatist is beyond them. The left immediately classifies the pragmatist as a corrupt and cold snake, slithering into success, without care for the oath of office or public interest, while the right believes that pragmatism is illusory. The pragmatist acts as if he is a benign count, requesting assistance with a real estate transaction, but in reality he is Dracula, the Prince of Darkness.

Donald Trump branded himself as a pragmatist – the dealmaker, the negotiator, the moneyman, etc. – but in reality he is the most ideological figure in American politics to emerge in many years. He is able to disguise his ideology of ruthless corporate calculation and white supremacy with America's social norms and cultural conventions, both of which authorize the Trump mentality.

While the right was fighting phantoms, and the left was busy in their administration of purity tests, the president was on the move to enact the most liberal reform agenda since the Great Society program of Lyndon B. Johnson. Like Ellison's narrator slipping in and out of an expensive apartment building, Obama snuck inside the mansion of American law, and rearranged the furniture. Had the right opposed the Obama that actually exists – the one that they could not see – they might have more successfully beat back his march into history. If the left celebrated his achievements, with more audible adulation, they might have alerted the right to his actual aim, and helped enable them to push it out of bounds. Instead with both right and left fighting over a president that does not exist, he was able to slip into the mansion past the sleeping guards.

In the 21st century, America remains a riddle few people can figure out. Never a country with a clear or definitive character, it is the battleground for people attempting to negotiate and navigate the collision between two equally powerful and real stories of America. It is the story of domination and democracy. It is the story of repression and revolution. It is the story of exploitation and equality. It is the story of dogma and dialogue. It is the immigrant arriving at American shores with dreams of liberty and independence fueling him down the superhighways of commerce and bureaucracy. It is the American plane dropping bombs that decimates the city of that immigrant's birth. As president, Obama contributed to both sides of the story. As a liberal reformer, he advanced the democratic and egalitarian side, always with an interest, even when it hurt him, in dialogue. As the commander-in-chief of an imperial military in the last gasp of empire, and as the face of political power, he also maintained the American tradition of dominion in foreign affairs. It is far too early to evaluate Obama's influence on the at once mighty and filigreed psyche of America. The ink of the tattoo he's made on American skin is not yet dry, and is not yet fully open to interpretation.

One of the few things that is certain is that the election of a living and breathing monument of multiculturalism, and a man who makes cheap puffery about diversity into magnificent reality – a black, white, African, American – is a triumph of the American story Whitman put to poetry long before many others could develop the maturity and imagination to understand its wisdom. In *Dreams from My Father*, thirteen years before he would become president-elect, Barack Obama, articulated and advanced his own rendition of Whitman's anthemic song, 'the voice of democracy.'

> 'We hold these truths to be self-evident.' In those words, I hear the spirit of Douglass and Delany, as well as Jefferson and Lincoln; the struggles of Martin and Malcolm and unheralded marchers to bring these words to life. I hear the voices of Japanese families interned behind barbed wire; young Russian Jews cutting patterns in Lower East Side sweatshops; dust bowl farmers loading up their trucks with the remains of shattered lives. I hear the voices of the people in Altgeld Gardens, and the voices of those who stand outside this country's borders, the weary, hungry bands crossing the Rio Grande. I hear all of these voices clamoring for recognition, all of them asking the very same questions that have come to shape my

> life... In the conversation itself, in the joining of voices, I find myself modestly encouraged, believing that so long as the questions are still being asked, what binds us together might somehow, ultimately, prevail.

The presidency of Obama – irrespective of its policies and by the measure of its existence – amplified the voice of democracy, and underscored the promise of its victory. There does exist the dream of the ties that bind withstanding the tornadic pull of ignorance and tribal hatred. The terms of unity often land with the thud of cliché, but it is a cliché worthy of faith. It is the cliché that Obama elevated into poetry when he aced his national audition giving the keynote address at the 2004 Democratic National Convention, and it is the cliché he embodied behind the presidential seal at the most prominent pulpit in the world. Millions of people on the political right and left could not accurately see Obama, because they cannot actually see America. It is a land of too much complexity and too many contradictions. Obama, like a literary invention Ellison could imagine, has become an archetypal representation of all of those contradictions – a characterized capsule busting at the edges.

The election of Donald Trump signals to the world that many Americans are not yet prepared for the full implications of America. Walt Whitman sold precious few books in his lifetime. In his essay, 'Democratic Vistas,' he worried that 'genuine belief had left' American culture. In its place existed only the cold and quixotic comfort of career advancement and material advantage. Over a century later, America has transitioned from Barack Obama – a learned, aspirational leader – to a man who presents America as nothing more than career advancement and material advantage. It is important, now more than ever, to consider the possibility that the idea of America is too radical even for most Americans. President Obama, not always politically, but culturally, more thoroughly captured the idea of America than any other modern president.

Of all the unanswerable and intractable questions that surround the Obama presidency and legacy, one conclusion is unavoidable for anyone with the intellectual honesty to look into the dark corridors of a personal and political belonging to a nation with an identity in constant flux and turmoil. It is the same conclusion Ellison's narrator reached when he wrote, 'Our fate is to become one, and yet many – This is not prophecy, but description. Thus one of the greatest jokes in the world is the spectacle of whites busy escaping blackness and becoming blacker every day, and the blacks striving toward whiteness, becoming quite dull and gray. None of us seems to know who he is or where he's going.'

Barack Obama is invisible, because to see him would require that we all see ourselves. It would demand that we finally unmask the face we wear that is at once full of breathtaking beauty, but also irredeemably ugly.

A MAN OF SUBSTANCE, FLESH, AND BONE

Analysts and activists in American politics have a deterministic tendency to strip presidents of personality, and depict them as sophisticated cyborgs acting in accordance with their corporate and Pentagon programming. It is important to acknowledge the influence of institutional incentives, financial pressures, and military power on the executive branch of the US government. President Eisenhower, in his farewell address to the nation, famously and presciently warned of the dangers emanating out of the 'military-industrial complex.' Big business colludes with big government at the level of campaign contributions, and even the most naïve voter would have to concede that those individuals or entities that can offer six figure donations will likely have more pull on the president than the ordinary voter writing a check for forty dollars. Every democracy must contend with the undue authority of undemocratic forces embedded in the government, but presidents are not actually characters from science fiction novels or dystopian movies. They are human beings who bring a human history, with all its complexity and contradiction, into the Oval Office. The personality and priorities formed out of this history also influence the creation of laws, execution of policies, and emphasis of ideas. It also produces tangible results in service or violation of the public will. President Clinton, with his holistic and nuanced appreciation for the subtleties of politics and policy, was in a much better position to govern as a clear-eyed and commanding leader than George W. Bush. Bush's historical ignorance and political fatuity made him an easy mark for the much savvier Donald Rumsfeld and Dick Cheney. The American people do not merely elect a machine fit for the tasks of corporate demand, even if corporate America has too loud of a voice in the public debate. The president, as banal as it sounds, is a person.

James David Barber, a political scientist, wrote in his groundbreaking study of presidential biography, *The Presidential Character*, that 'The lives of presidents past and of the one still with us show how a start from character makes possible a realistic estimate of what will endure into a man's White House years...Character is the force, the motive power, around which the person gathers his view of the world, and from which his style receives its impetus. The issues will change; the character of the president will not.' Years prior to Nixon's decline into paranoia, lawlessness, and hysteria bordering on mental illness, Barber predicted that he would end his presidency with impeachment or resignation. The biographical details of Nixon's travail into power revealed that he was a rigid, aggressive, and delusional man who would not enjoy the altruistic aspects of his position, but would view his authority as primarily a therapeutic tool for self-actualization. Barack Obama is much different.

Far from a demonic cartoon villain or soulless symbol of political purity destined for failure, Obama is what Ellison's protagonist called, 'a man of substance, of flesh and bone, fiber and liquids.' 'I might even be said to possess a mind,' he went on to write. It is impossible to understand the presidency of Barack Obama, or the person who became president, without gaining insight into Obama's life, and the experiences that formed his character. The figure that emerges, even from a cursory sketch, is complicated, but impressive; elusive, but fascinating. The contradictory character of Obama obstructs visibility into his personality. As America becomes less intellectually sophisticated and increasingly polarized, people have the temptation to constantly classify everyone and everything as good or evil. The Manichean worldview does not allow for the recognition of human complexity. Obama's story is complicated, and the man who emerges from that story is a rich archetype of American achievement. Much of the American public ignored the substance behind the symbol, and muted the mind of the man in the Oval Office. Had they closely studied the triumphs and turning points that led him to Washington D.C., they would have had more reasonable expectations of his presidential performance, and demonstrated an intelligent reaction to his agenda and ambition.

Like most presidents, a wealth of information exists on Obama's life, but the best starting point is the one coordinated by the man himself in his artistic memoir, *Dreams from My Father*. Written in the style and with the skill of a novelist and published in 1995, *Dreams from My Father* is an intense character study of a conflicted and talented figure attempting to engage in the art of self-discovery, even as his childhood, family, and the racial politics of America conspire to make it difficult and painful. The book is not one someone expecting to run for high office would write, as it is full of potentially damaging confessions, and much too subtle for a mass audience. Obama wrote it after receiving a publishing deal, because of his election as first black president – not of the nation, but of the *Harvard Law Review*. He planned to write an essay collection about issues of race, public policy, and law, but soon found that his political and legal philosophy was inseparable from his own identity. As he attempted to explicate legal theory, he found himself continually distracted by reflections on his upbringing, and his search for self-awareness. Alone in the modern presidency, Obama, prior to political fame, wrote what is now a classic book of the African American, memoir, and creative nonfiction genres. The character of Barack, full of precocious wisdom but also bitter with resentment toward his father, instantly resembles any young person who has struggled to find footing in a world that so often seems to shift underneath their feet. With each revelation about race, ancestry, or American democracy, Obama is able to locate a sign of self-direction within his own spirit. There is an ethnic and geographic particularity to his story, but like great stories, and like all great storytellers, Obama finds the universality within specificity. Literary accomplishment for an American politician is rare, but Obama made a masterful contribution to the memoir of personal exploration. 'The unexamined life is not worth living,' Socrates famously warned. In *Dreams from My Father*, Obama examines his life, and gives the reader an opportunity to explore the nuances of race, diversity, and identity in a nation where those things are always in collision and negotiation.

It is instructive, and an exercise in depression, to compare Obama's artistic finesse with the hideous and hollow book of Donald Trump's claim to fame. Barack Obama wrote his memoir without any assistance from a ghostwriter, while Trump merely dictated vague thoughts on business and celebrity to a writer, who would later call Trump 'sociopathic,' for *The Art of the Deal*.[1] Trump's bestseller is philosophically and ethically empty – a tribute to nothing more than winning at all costs and gaining financial advantage even if it requires manipulation and exploitation of other people. The polar opposite, Obama's book is about a lonely man's struggle to develop self-awareness, and in the process find a communal mechanism for him to put his intellect and talent to use for the benefit of others.

Through the turbulence of self-discovery, Obama transformed from a dejected and detached cynic into a man of motion more faithful in small and steady acts of improvement than grandiose gestures of symbolic value. His life would soon find itself subsumed in irony, as his election as first black president was the grandest gesture of symbolism imaginable, but his actual presidency – much to the dismay and chagrin of many supporters – was a pragmatic exercise in levelheaded reform. Long before his political ascendancy, he would transition into what Barber called an 'active-positive' presidential personality. An active-positive president, like John Kennedy, Jimmy Carter, or Bill Clinton, demonstrates an overall readiness to act, optimism about his ability to govern and the nation's future, and an enthusiasm for the ceremonial, administrative, and communicative components of the job. Much to the surprise of Americans who found themselves in awe of his oratory, Obama, in his first term, seemed to show less enthusiasm for the rhetorical aspects of the presidency than he did for the actual diligence of governance. This reversal of the image he projected in 2008 surprised both admirers, who thought he would persuade the nation into a nearly universal adoption of liberalism, and detractors, who believed he was nothing but a sophist masking his naiveté and incompetence with a series of well-timed, well-delivered speeches. Anyone who actually bothered to look into the early adult life of Obama, along with his legislative activity in the Illinois State Senate and the United States Senate, would have known that he had much more of a quiet, workmanlike approach than he otherwise appeared. It is manipulative to talk about talent in relation to art or politics, because it denies, or at least, shadows the essentiality of labor. Talent without dedication to craft is nothing more than a missed opportunity. Obama, like many influential artists and administrators, talks like a dreamer, but lives as a worker.

The 'dreams' from Obama's father were the aspirational dreams of personal glory and political greatness; the hope that one could rise above limits of ethnicity, culture, and politics to create a life of value, and use that creation to empower the lives of other people with similar goals. Barack Obama, Senior, loomed large in the mind and faith of his son, mainly because he lived across an ocean, thousands of miles away. Obama knew his father for a total of two weeks, when he stayed with him in Hawaii before retreating back to Kenya to remain under familial concealment until his early death. Eventually, Obama would learn that the tower he constructed in the pantheon of his mind – a genius with a Harvard education, an important and influential man of power in the Kenyan government – was only partially representational. In reality, as Obama would learn from his siblings who knew the man in Africa, he was a bitter drunk, disappointed with his bureaucratic position, and all too willing to exercise his frustrations through the cruel catharsis of spousal abuse. When he learned the true nature of his father's character, he didn't know whether to cry or laugh. He felt like a 'drunk coming out of a long binge' – the terror and freedom of sobriety confronting him at once. It was the resolve and stability of other ancestors and familial figures that actually informed his behavior, especially once the invention of a heroic, but absent father could not withstand the scrutiny of the truth. The spiritual death and disappearance of a hero, for the person who has gained sufficient wisdom to progress in the wake of the loss, does not necessitate the substitution of a new hero, but the realization that heroes are almost always the fragments of lost myths. To replace the faded hero, one must become his own hero, but such work is impossible without the affirmation of mere mortals who can imbue a life with love and trust.

Obama explains his admiration for his grandmother as a natural response to her wisdom, and it is wisdom never too far from the ground. She is 'suspicious of overwrought sentiments and overblown claims,' and she is 'content with common sense' – the exact opposite of the characteristics, ungrounded faith, and fantasy Obama relied upon to struggle through the childhood absence of his father. He writes that one of the renewable sources of energy for his grandmother, through a tough life, was the 'stoicism of her ancestors.' His grandmother's daughter – his own mother – would have an even more influential impact on his life. Obama describes his mother's altruism, political passion, and commitment to causes of justice with the pragmatic terminology of the Enlightenment and the philosophy of the social contract:

> My mother's confidence in needlepoint virtues depended on a faith I didn't possess, a faith that she would refuse to describe as religious; that, in fact, her experience told her was sacrilegious: a faith that rational, thoughtful people could shape their own

> destiny. In a land where fatalism remained a necessary tool for enduring hardship, where ultimate truths were kept separate from day-to-day realities, she was a lonely witness for secular humanism, a soldier for New Deal, Peace Corps, position-paper liberalism.

Writing that sentence, Obama also described his younger self, and the days when he belonged to the 'club of the disaffected.' How he gave birth to his own faith in the miracle of rationality, and how he became not only a soldier, but a general for position-paper liberalism, provides the narrative heart of *Dreams from My Father* – a book that doubles as a born again testimony of a man who elevated himself above the easy to access, dry dirt of cynicism, toward the higher ground of hope – hope not through prayer and ritual, but hope through the active theology of Frederick Douglass, who in his work to abolish slavery, explained that his prayers were never answered until he prayed with his feet. The cynicism that disaffection breeds is paralytic. Only hope can quicken the steps of the prayerful, and provide the power source for the work that builds, rather than breaks. Had Obama never adopted his mother's secular faith, he might have never made it out of the club. He certainly would not have become president of the United States.

Obama began praying with his feet while walking through the blight and obliteration, and among the crime and poverty, of Chicago's war-weary Southside neighborhoods. He accepted a position as a community organizer, and found himself with the unenviable task of trying to mobilize residents struggling against the hardships of their own existence – bills getting bigger while the paychecks stay the same, bullets finding their way into the breasts of loved ones. The causes were clear: trying to recruit entrepreneurs and manufacturers to open shops on the Southside, attempting to pressure police to better control crime without resorting to racial profiling, and improve the efficacy of the largely dysfunctional public schools. Before he became a community organizer, however, he entered that interim and awkward stage between disaffection and dedication. He became interested in politics, and curious about using the instruments of institutional policies to help people, but refocused his cynicism into a steely skepticism against the possibility of any change. In a brilliant stroke of irony, fit for literary invention, Barack, as a detached and sanctimonious cynic, was precisely the insufferable style of leftist he would fight as Obama, liberal president.

Obama writes about his mother and sister visiting him in New York, while he was earning his undergraduate degree at Columbia University. With embarrassment, he remembers scolding his sister for watching television instead of reading about the serious ideas she claimed to cherish. He condescended to his mother about her decision to work for a philanthropic organization in Africa, claiming that they 'breed dependence' and cannot address the structural inequality separating the two poles of the globe. 'Barack's OK, isn't he?' Obama remembers hearing his sister ask his mother when they thought he was asleep, 'I mean, I hope he doesn't lose his cool and become one of those freaks you see on the streets around here.'

The death of Obama's father, along with the destruction of his illusion, seemed to emancipate him from extremity, and release him into the rational. He went from believing that nothing is possible to accepting that small changes are indeed possible, and that small changes are the building blocks of big change. He became a community organizer in the 1980s, because he believed that change from the White House was impossible – 'Reagan and his minions were carrying out their dirty deeds' – change from a 'corrupt and compliant' Congress was equally unlikely, and that the mood of the country was also an obstacle, as it was becoming increasingly 'manic and self-absorbed.' Hindsight allowed Obama to realize that his early career choice was not his alone, but part of a larger narrative starting with his father and his father before him, his mother and her parents, and his memories of Indonesia with its beggars and farmers. Obama's cosmopolitan stoicism seemed to inform him of the differences between Third World catastrophes and 'First World problems,' but it also taught him that problems are problems, and that they all cry out for solutions.

Gore Vidal once defined an intellectual as someone who can 'deal with abstractions.' Intellectual analysis of any problem is important, and it is especially worthy of advocacy in the United States, which for decades has cultivated an anti-intellectual culture. There is certain wisdom to gain, however, from the on-the-ground application of theory. To observe the success or failure of an abstraction applied to the everyday is to gain a more intimate form of confidence in the validity or vacuity of an idea. Obama's baptism by fire in the scorched streets of Chicago allowed him to engineer a bridge between intellect and action. The sacramental act, like the destruction of the false idol he constructed out of the scattered pieces of his father's image, led him not into the arms of doctrinal prescription, but into a whirlwind of confusion. It is within that confusion that committed people grab at answers, and sometimes even in a shock to themselves, return home with something in hand.

Early in his experience as an organizer, Obama identified himself – standing in an empty parking lot of a McDonald's on a windy day in the windy city – as a 'heretic.' He was a 'heretic' against the complementary dogmas of politics and religion. 'In politics, like religion,' Obama writes, 'power lay in certainty – and one man's certainty always threatens another's.'

According to Obama, it is in devotion to the faith claims that certainty requires that people reject compromise, and resist any information presenting a more complex and nuanced depiction of the world than what they have come to believe. In his presidency Obama would advance his heresy against the dogmatic right, committed to the belief that he was an anti-American saboteur, and the dogmatic left, devoted to the dogma that he was a helpless sell out, but in Chicago he met earlier prototypes of the doctrinaire. There were the elderly residents of the Southside who, still dealing with the trauma of Jim Crow, believed that all of their neighborhood's problems were the result of nothing more than 'devious white aldermen' and bigoted white policemen. Then, there was Rafiq – a black nationalist Muslim – who served as a cautionary tale against the pitfalls and paralysis of extreme ideology. As a foot soldier for Louis Farrakhan, Rafiq spoke with passion, but soon exposed himself – and his fellow travelers – as hopelessly passive. Black nationalism, Obama writes, 'can thrive as an emotion, but will flounder as a program.' It offers only catharsis, and in doing so, it might 'win the applause of the jobless teenager listening on the radio or the businessman watching late-night TV,' but it will fail to answer the questions most fundamental to beleaguered black people's lives. A black accountant, after hearing Farrakhan's thunderous appeal for financial separatism, will ask, 'How am I going to open an account at the black-owned bank if it charges me extra for checking and won't even give me a business loan because it says it can't afford the risk?' The black nurse will listen to a black Muslim demand that she put her skills to service solely for other African Americans, and she will think, 'White folks I work with ain't so bad, and even if they were, I can't be quitting my job – who's gonna pay my rent tomorrow, or feed my child today?'

Obama recalls Rafiq sputtering out predictable clichés when faced with such obvious inquiries. It is not merely black nationalism that Obama learned was fated for failure, but all forms of idealistic purity. An effective leader, organizer, or reformer must work with the world as it presents itself, and as it exists, not with the world he dreams might exist in some distant, utopic future. The 'invisible man' of Ellison's creation also learns of the duplicity and dangers of black nationalism through his encounters with Ras the Destroyer, a demagogue inspired by Marcus Garvey. As Ellison's narrator struggles to learn how he can invest his time and talent into the improvement of living conditions for black residents of New York City, all Ras can offer is fiery speeches about the evils of white society. Even when he accurately diagnoses the problem – the institutions of white society were predatory and poisonous in the 1950s – he has no effective treatment or curative prescription. He has only the bombastic delivery of his screaming rhetoric. The results-driven, reform emphasis of Obama's approach to political organization and public policy emerged over time as he observed the power of subtle successes in the Southside of Chicago, where even minor differences can account for major effects in poverty-stricken and crime-ridden neighborhoods. The political mathematics of minor differences equaling major effects took on more appeal to Obama than the sorcery of Ras, and many one note leftists, who seem to believe that anything less than the always unrealistic revolution betrays the principles of freedom and justice.

The act of investigating his own memories allowed Obama to realize when he experienced an epiphany. It was not winning an election, or receiving minor publicity as the first black president of the *Harvard Law Review*. It was nothing so glamorous. A group of poor, black mothers, acting with the assistance of Obama as organizer, took a bus to the Chicago Housing Authority office to confront the agency's director over why there was uncertainty as to whether or not the public housing units where they lived had undergone testing for asbestos. Obama had alerted some reporters to the planned confrontation, and when the CHA's director sent out a press lackey who tried to obfuscate the issue with platitudes, Obama stepped back and watched the mothers pin her down to an answer, all while a handful of journalists recorded every word. At the end of the brief, but relentless interrogation, the spokeswoman for the CHA admitted that they had never conducted asbestos tests, even though they are mandated by law, but agreed to have testing begin the next day. She also arranged for a meeting with the director to discuss the results of the tests. Obama describes the quiet, but substantial victory as transformative.

> I changed as a result of that bus trip, in a fundamental way. It was the sort of change that's important not because it alters your concrete circumstances in some

> way (wealth, security, fame) but because it hints at what might be possible and therefore spurs you on, beyond the immediate exhilaration, beyond any subsequent disappointments, to retrieve that thing that you once, ever so briefly, held in your hand. That bus ride kept me going. Maybe it still does.

Idealistic purity produces nothing but temper tantrums and self-directed gestures of outrage, while real world action, even when softened by compromise or concession, enhances the quality of life for suffering people – easing their pain and brightening their futures. The enhancement of their quality of life, gave them the only justification that they needed to make Barack Obama a beloved figure in their community. When Obama returned to give a speech to the beleaguered group, while home from Harvard Law, he sermonized the sweet success of the small step. The mothers, activists, and residents were enraged, because the city had denied them a permit to build a community center, but approved funding for communal programs should they ever purchase property and open the institution. Rather than interpreting it solely as the dirty trick and runaround that it likely was, Obama, always on assignment for pragmatic hope, told them to use the funding for ammunition to acquire the sponsorship and support of local organizations and businesses. Then, they could return to the city council with the pressures, incentives, and devices of manipulation all too necessary for political persuasion. Obama's legislation and leadership, locally and nationally, followed the familiar formula, if paradoxical, of starry-eyed realism.

The senatorial career – first at the state level and then in a single term at the federal level – of Barack Obama compiles into a portfolio of pragmatic achievement. In his tenure in the Illinois State Senate, he shepherded a law through the chamber that prohibited state legislators from accepting gifts from lobbyists, and from using campaign funds for personal purposes. It certainly would not end all corruption or eliminate undue influence from donors, but it would reduce the instruments of corruption, and increase the incentives for public transparency and honesty. He co-sponsored a bill to restructure the state's welfare payment system to resemble the federal process, in order to enhance efficiency, and he championed legislation to increase childcare subsidies for low-income families. These legislative achievements would not end poverty, but they would reduce the pain of poverty by making it a little easier for poor parents to get to work, take care of their children, and stock the refrigerator. Later he would expand government funds for children's health care, oversee the creation of a 'Hospital Report Card' evaluation system enabling patients and families to give ratings to medicinal facilities. Such a maneuver would fail to address every crisis in the inefficient and unjust American health care system, but it would save lives. Perhaps his most significant accomplishment at the state level was when he wrote and was responsible for the passage of a bill requiring police officers to videotape all interrogations and confessions in potential death penalty cases, saving more lives and making another small, but considerable dent in the wall of human suffering. None of Obama's state accomplishments were radical acts, but he never advertised himself as a radical.

Barack Obama won political promotion in 2004. After a devastating defeat in an election for a Congressional seat, he adopted what he calls an 'up or out strategy.' He ran for the United States Senate, and assured his wife, increasingly frustrated by having to compete with voters for her husband's attention, that if he did not win the race, and it looked as if the odds of success were low, he would permanently retire from politics to teach law on a full time basis at the University of Chicago, where he was already a lecturer, or open a civil rights law firm. The 'up' element of his strategy turned into reality after a series of unpredictable and beneficial developments set up a scaffold for his unlikely victory. First, his charismatic and popular opponent dropped out of the race because of a sex scandal, and second, the Republican party thought it was a good idea to replace him with Alan Keyes, a carpetbagger from New York who accused Obama of contributing to a 'culture of evil' by supporting the legal status of abortion, and condemned all gay people as 'selfish hedonists.' The irrationality and extremity of Keyes, demonstrated most clearly when he refused to congratulate Obama on his authoritative victory, offered a preview of the opposition Obama would face as president. Unfortunately, the maniacs of the modern Republican Party would not prove so easy to silence for President Obama.

Before Obama became the leader of America's executive branch of government, he would introduce himself to the entire country with a keynote address at the 2004 Democratic National Convention. The reaction to his national audition was so overwhelming, and unanimous, that speculation about this eventual presidency began the next morning. It was both a launch and a weight for Obama – a launch for the obvious reason that he inspired millions of people, across ideological lines, with his stirring tribute to the multiculturalist prospect of unity in American life, but a weight because many people would always hold him to such a high standard. As president, Obama was often criticized for his supposed 'failure to bring people together,' and such critics will typically refer to his keynote speech to measure the distance between his promise and performance. Obama possesses no divine powers, and without the ability to engineer miracles, it always seemed unlikely that he could unify a nation showing signs of its worst polarization since the Civil War, and crashing into a brick wall due to the misdirection of increasingly demented right wing navigation. The eventual election of Donald Trump to the presidency proves that Obama had no real chance of organizing the unification of the increasingly fractured American people. What could Obama have done to persuade and appeal to people who believe he is an evil agent of Satan, and would welcome the prospect of a vulgar and boorish bigot taking residence in the White House?

Much of the villainous casting of Obama is dependent upon spotlighting his cosmopolitan background, and biracial status, to imagine him as alternative to America. His 2004 speech – likely one of the greatest in convention history despite its maudlin excesses – was a tribute to America, as emotional as it was political. Referencing the founding fathers, ambitious and courageous immigrants, Martin Luther King, and ordinary citizens he met on the campaign trail, he used poetic rhetoric, and gospel oratory, to amplify the Whitman vision of unity from diversity. His most popular line of the evening, and now most recited, is the simple declaration, 'there's not a liberal

America and a conservative America – there's the United States of America. There's not a black America and white America and Latino America and Asian America; there's the United States of America.' Barack Obama blends biography and sociology to provide an anatomy of inspiration for the sentiment in his book, *The Audacity of Hope*. He emerges as an archetypal representative of American identity, which is always in a steady and chaotic process of multiplication and fluctuation:

> In a sense, I have no choice but to believe in this vision of America. As a child of a black man and white woman, someone who was born in the racial melting pot of Hawaii, with a sister who's half Indonesian but who's usually mistaken for Mexican or Puerto Rican, and a brother-in-law and niece of Chinese descent, with some blood relatives who resemble Margaret Thatcher and others who could pass for Bernie Mac, so that family get-togethers over Christmas take on the appearance of a UN General Assembly meeting, I've never had the option of restricting my loyalties on the basis of race, or measuring my worth on the basis of tribe.

Chris Matthews, former speechwriter for President Carter and current host of the MSNBC political talk show *Hardball*, has suffered significant embarrassment and mockery for his immediate on air reaction to the speech. He announced that during its most triumphant moments, he 'felt a thrill run up his leg.' [2] The sexual undertones in his poor choice of words mask the true meaning of the endorsement. Matthews was referring to the power of inspiration, something that had vanished from American politics after Dr. King and the Kennedy brothers were assassinated, and had not reappeared in decades. Nixon probably had difficulty inspiring his own family. Carter attempted to provoke America into a more mature outlook, but did so with an ineffective style. Reagan's supporters found him inspirational in the 1980s, but the ease with which he targeted liberals with invective nullified his potential into partisan dispute. Clinton spoke with hopeful tones and charismatic delivery, but by the time of his arrival, the cultural divide already seemed unbreachable. Obama emerged in the context of the George W. Bush presidency – a hideous fiasco he rightly labeled, near the end of his address, a 'period of political darkness.' It was the inspirational efficacy of Obama – the reawakening of an optimistic and hopeful spirit inherent in his story and delivery – that made millions of people speculate, as premature as it seemed, that soon this newly elected senator with an Arabic name would become the nation's first black president. It was a triumphant, but ultimately misleading debut. Obama's reformative ambitions, in the Senate Chamber and Oval Office, as even he wrote about his accomplishments of his single term in the United States Senate, were modest: 'None of these amendments would transform the country, but I took satisfaction in knowing that each of them helped some people in a modest way or nudged the law in a direction that might prove to be more economical, more responsible, or more just.'

Obama's reference in that honest assessment of his legislative career is to the amendments he authored in three years: Additional funds for programs designed to help homeless parents, tax credits to gas stations for installing E85 fuel pumps, and the elimination of no-bid contracts in the post-Katrina reconstruction of New Orleans. Obama also co-wrote a bill with veteran Republican, Richard Lugar of Indiana, to restrict weapons proliferation and black market arms trading. A credible argument against Obama's election to the presidency in 2008 was his lack of experience in national politics and policymaking. One of the ways in which the always-graceful Obama was able to counterpunch this complaint was recitation of his resume in the Illinois Senate and US Senate. Despite only serving one term, he distinguished himself as a pragmatic actor with an active mind; a politician who examines problems, develops workable solutions, and ushers those solutions out of the domain of philosophical fantasy and into the political reality. The reality, however, is always a tight space with a door that's difficult to unlock.

Much of the modesty of Obama's achievements as senator, and later as president, is a result of systemic limitations no leader, no matter how brilliant and charismatic, can overcome. Triumvirate government, according to the design of the Constitutional framers, imposes restrictions on power, and makes reform difficult so as to ensure that no executive or Congressional body can have too strong an influence over America's law, politics, or future. When frustrated voters throw their hands in the air and complain that the government 'never gets anything done,' they often betray a misunderstanding of civics. No president, under the restraint of checks and balances, is supposed to get much done. The mandate for dysfunction is simultaneously one of the American government's greatest features and flaws. It prevents misuse of power, infringement on personal liberty and choice, and an excess of governmental expansion. At the same time, it also acts as unmovable congestion stalling, and often obstructing, political movement in the direction of necessary improvement. In addition to constitutional limits on power, there also exists institutional corruption, and the undemocratic authority of embedded interests at various levels of government. In the Oliver Stone film, *Nixon*, the cinematic version of the disgraced president refers to the state-corporate-intelligence nexus surrounding him, and narrowing his options for decision-making, as a 'beast.' [3] The dramatic language of Stone – one of America's great dramatists – is accurate in its identification of personal and policy pressures on the president, not immediately visible to the public eye. It becomes a wild animal, because without the leash of the electorate, it is nearly impossible to control. The State Department, the Central Intelligence Agency, and the Department of Defense, to use three particularly powerful examples, all have an agenda of self-interest, and the unelected officials and bureaucrats who staff those offices do their best to exert their agenda on the will of elected government. On top of those layers of limit, Obama had to contend with unprecedented opposition from a borderline insane Republican Congress, barely willing to acknowledge that Obama is a human being, much less collaborate with him on policy authorship and implementation. If the founders intended for legal and political reforms to take place only after lengthy negotiation and compromise from the multiple levels of governance, Obama had to lead with one arm tied behind his back, and one branch sawed off the tree.

The presidential personality still makes an impact on the presidential record, however. As much as Obama deserves adulation for the clarity of his pragmatism, he also deserves condemnation for an element of cowardice in his conciliation.

Few political figures have so eloquently and convincingly criticized the shortcomings of pragmatism as Barack Obama himself. 'The best I can do in the face of our history is remind myself,' Obama wrote, 'that it has not always been the pragmatist, the voice of reason, or the force of compromise, that has created the conditions for liberty. The hard, cold facts remind me that it was the unbending idealists like William Lloyd Garrison who first sounded the clarion call for justice; that it was slaves and former slaves, men like Denmark Vesey and Frederick Douglass and women like Harriet Tubman, who recognized power would concede nothing without a fight.' The brave fight Obama is waging against himself on the page becomes palpable, especially in its closing moments when he offers a conclusion so unforgiving it is almost an exercise in self-directed brutality: 'The blood of the slaves reminds us that our pragmatism can sometimes be moral cowardice.'

If there is one thing that seems to make Obama suspicious and uncomfortable, it is certainty. Throughout his two books, he continues to return to his natural tendency toward skepticism, his comfort in contradiction, and his belief that danger is inherent in absolute belief. In a postmodern twist, he claims that he cannot even take certainty in uncertainty – 'I am robbed of the certainty of uncertainty – for sometimes absolute truths may very well be absolute.' From a moral and political standpoint, the rejection of absolute truth and dogmatic certainty places Obama far outside the American center. When George W. Bush condemned 'evildoers,' and paraphrased Jesus Christ, by warning foreign nations, 'You are either with us or against us,' he represented the prevalent American worldview: Manichean, uncomplicated, and uncompromising. Much of the dichotomous categorization in America results from religious devotion. Americans demonstrate greater belief in gods, devils, demons, and angels than the people of any other educated country. A civil theology then develops out of the prayers and superstition of Americans in which America becomes a godly force operating under a heavenly banner. Its enemies – communists, Vietnamese, Muslims – are minions of the devil without redemptive values or human characteristics. It seems more than coincidental that Obama, who was an atheist into his twenties, rejects such a static perspective. As president, he would often acknowledge atheists in addresses on religion and culture, and in one of his first international acts, he gave a speech in Cairo to address America's offenses against the Muslim world.

Obama considers himself a student and acolyte of Abraham Lincoln, another president who had a conflicted relationship with religion. The affinity makes sense, given that Lincoln's ideology is best understood as, what literary critic John Burt calls, 'tragic pragmatism.' Tragic pragmatism, according to the Burt definition, is the awareness that, even when demands are imperative and absolute, 'we are required to practice the art of the possible in realizing them, always wagering that our compromises will not somehow compromise them.' Obama, in simpler language, credits Lincoln with possessing an unmatched understanding of 'the deliberative function of our democracy and the limits of such deliberation.'

Barack Obama, as community organizer, state senator, US senator, and president, demonstrated an active-positive personality in his enthusiasm for passing reforms, changing institutional procedure, and diligently dedicating himself to the labor of governance, but his embrace of uncertainty went beyond pragmatism, even of the tragic variety, and became an all-encompassing faith in limits. In this sense, he is deeply conservative. Lincoln feared making bold moves, because he was attempting to prevent the outbreak of a civil war. With good reason, he believed that America would never recover from such internal and bloody battle. Although the stakes are high for any president, Obama could never claim that American survival hung in the balance of his health care reform initiative, or his plans to engineer economic recovery, even if they were and are undeniably important and impressive.

It is fairly common to see apparel and posters with the faces of Barack Obama and Martin Luther King, Jr., together. King and Obama are the most recognizable and transformational black male leaders of modern American history, but their respective ideologies, analyses of power, and approaches to political reform, are dramatically different. President Obama, like any good liberal, believed in the instruments of official governance, and sought to manipulate them for the common good. The results of activist legislation are significant – the establishment and protection of the middle class, the expansion of public medicine, the improvement of public schools – but they appear at the end of a process that moves at a glacial pace. Winston Churchill once remarked, 'You can always count on Americans to do the right thing, after they've tried everything else.' Obama, with a realism that rejects both cynicism and idealism, accepted that progress in the public interest of justice is gradual and incremental. King was a vociferous and courageous critic of such a slow maneuver in the direction of what is right. 'We have also come to this hallowed spot to remind America of the fierce urgency of now,' he announced during his 'I Have a Dream' speech in

1963. 'This is no time to engage in the luxury of cooling off or to take the tranquilizing drug of gradualism.'

Although King worked with JFK and LBJ to adjust the institutional procedure of power, he led a movement to pressure those presidents into cooperation. King understood the wisdom of Vladimir Lenin, who believed that power exists in the street waiting for someone capable to pick it up. The dichotomy between bureaucratic machination and populist revolution is the contrast between King and Obama. Reality was never lost on Obama, who, despite referencing King in his masterful 'Yes We Can' speech, never compared himself to the civil rights leader and martyr. When an interviewer asked if King would have endorsed his historic candidacy in 2008, Obama explained that King, if alive, would not endorse any candidacy. Instead, he would 'call upon the American people into arguing, mobilizing, agitating, and ultimately force elected officials to be accountable.'

One of the problems with President Barack Obama is that there weren't nearly enough community organizer Barack Obamas mobilizing a movement to enlarge his political ambitions, and aim for grander achievements. The survival of any republic demands the participation of an informed, intelligent, and engaged citizenry. Black Lives Matter, the fight for fifteen activists, and the burgeoning environmental movement offer signs of hope, but the Tea Party, the NRA, and the Trump coalition reawaken old fears, best captured by Sinclair Lewis, that a revolution from the right is much likelier than radical change from the left in America. The reality is that Obama's accomplishments and alterations of American law and culture, for all of their substantive significance, emerge as fragments of a beautiful picture not yet brought into existence.

The always-troublesome question of how best to organize the left and add to its numbers returns with new resonance. It is a question that Barack Obama, as community organizer, was seeking to answer, but as president, operating in an institutional role, neglected. Politically, just as psychologically, there are two halves to Obama. The psychological dichotomy becomes clear with consideration that for someone who spent most of his life as a public figure, he still remains elusive – not in a dangerous or diabolical way, as the right would allege, but in a way that certainly separates him from the what-you-see-is-what-you-get George W. Bush, or the constantly confessional Bill Clinton.

It might seem contradictory to make a claim that a president has not dedicated himself to public service, but unlike King, whose heroic life was directed outward, much of Obama's life seems to have an inward direction. *Dreams from My Father* shows a man whose biggest battles take place in the war theater of the soul, and the only area of life in which Obama seems to claim confidence in certainty is his family. Barack Obama was not just the first black president; he was also the father in the first black presidential family. Obama's wife, Michelle, who, in many ways is equally or more impressive than him, and their two daughters, Malia and Sasha, were also White House residents. The family maintained an elegance and integrity throughout their two terms that, perhaps better than any argument, exposed the evil stupidity of stereotypes against black people, and shamed lesser whites into evaluation of their own faith in white superiority. The strength of the solidarity of the Obama clan is an illustration of Christopher Lasch's definition of the family as a 'haven in a heartless world.' Like any introvert, Obama appears to take refuge in his own internal life, and in the interior world of his familial sanctuary. He does not seem to grab at enrichment in the outside world, but searches for it in the same source of his nourishment. *Dreams from My Father*, despite its triumphant ending, is a sad autopsy of the effects of a broken family. Much of Obama's struggle was the struggle to overcome the pain and doubt of patriarchal abandonment and neglect. There is a moving scene in the memoir in which Obama recalls a conversation with a colleague who offers nothing but praise for his own father. 'Your dad was always there for you?' Obama asks. When his colleague answers in the affirmative, Obama follows up with another question, 'Do you ever tell him 'thank you'?' 'Not really,' the coworker and friend answers. 'You should call him tonight and say 'thank you,'' Obama advises with words only the wounded can truly understand.

In his long search for the shelter of familial structure, Obama learned he had to act as his own architect and construction crew. The love of his wife and daughters is the result of his love and labor. Obama invested such an abundance of energy in his own house that the White House, as odd as it seems, might have become secondary. He governed with an active-positive faith in position-paper liberalism, but acquired the healthy detachment from his job that Nixon, who manipulated the instruments of power for his therapeutic ends, tragically lacked. Obama, more than other presidents, seems to benefit from the hard fought acquiescence of self-awareness. He empties himself out most thoroughly to his family, and everyone else – including the American people – remain at a distance. It is a distance that is at once compelling and frustrating for most observers, and it is a distance Obama himself had to learn to selectively overcome to effectively communicate to those on the outside of his haven in a heartless world.

It would shock many Obama voters, and even many of his detractors, to learn that one of the reasons he lost his first election for national office was because of his unappealing speaking style. His oratory was overly academic, and he struggled to connect with constituents at the unmapped meeting ground of emotion. A prominent member of the Chicago black business world, and a day one Obama supporter, took him to meet with Jesse Jackson, and asked if the former aide to Dr. King and former presidential candidate who nearly became the first black nominee twenty years before Obama in 1988, would coach and counsel him on his rhetorical delivery. Jackson's Democratic Convention speeches from 1984 and 1988 remain powerful to the point of awe. Having Jackson as a speech instructor is the equivalent of having Babe Ruth show a minor leaguer how to swing a bat.

Jackson saw great potential in the state senator, but they met only once. During that meeting Obama told Jackson that when he saw his stellar performance in the 1980s, Democratic primary debates, as a college student, he thought to himself, in reference to the possibility of a black president – 'This thing can happen.' One of the most profound images of the triumphant night that Obama became president-elect is that of Jesse Jackson – a man who politically and personally helped make the possibility of a black president into reality – unable to hold back the flood of tears from his eyes. Awaiting the victory speech, Jackson explained that he cried for 'the moment and the movement.' The moment made him cry tears of joy, but the movement made him cry tears of pain for all of those who labored, bled, and died to make it happen, but could not stand beside him to enjoy it.[4]

President Obama is a child of the movement. Whether he becomes the father of a movement remains an unanswered question. What is immediately clear is that he is a fascinating character of the American drama – one that refuses to surrender to any stereotype or conform to central casting. He is not Jesse Jackson. He is not Martin Luther King. He is not a messiah. He is not a monster. He is Barack Obama. He is a singular human being in possession of all the characteristics, complications, and contradictions that one identity manages to pull into a cohesive whole.

In his apologia for *Invisible Man,* Ellison wrote that part of his purpose was to 'reveal the human complexity which stereotypes are intended to conceal.' A tragic contradiction of the American experience in the 21st century is that the American people twice elected a man president who they could not see through a concealment of their own design.

THESE UNITED STATES

It is impossible to understand any president of the United States of America without first gaining some comprehension of America. The torture of that task awaiting any philosopher or historian is that America, existing as a singular and odd entity in global history and identity, is nearly impossible to understand. First, the inevitable identification of contradiction riddles any diagnosis of national condition with error. America is Martin Luther King, but it also the burning cross, the white sheet robe, and the blunt force trauma of the nightstick against the black skull. America is Elvis Presley, the birth of rock 'n' roll, and the Summer of Love, but it is also the church usher, the virginity pledge, and the stale abstinence-only sex-ed classroom. America is the land of opportunity where immigrants from all over the world travel to open their own shop on the corner, but it is also the mediocrity of mass culture, Madison Avenue, and the corporate boardroom. America is Main Street and Wall Street. It is the promise of freedom, and the stench of death rising from a bomb crater in a Third World country. America is both a bride in white smiling through her nuptial vows, and a whip-cracking mistress in a black leather jumpsuit.

Those brave and brilliant artists who have attempted to figure out America, even in their most triumphant moments, have only scratched the surface. It is a strange and silly country that somehow manages to scintillate with the sensation of sex, wealth, rebellion, excitement, and pleasure. 'Life, liberty, and the pursuit of happiness' means a million different things to a million different people, and that is precisely why America produces preachers as divergent as Pat Robertson and Jesse Jackson, entertainers as opposite as Beyoncé and Barbra Streisand, and presidents as different as Donald Trump and Barack Obama. America is a mystery no detective could solve. It is a crime without clues, and a gift of grace without precedent. It is a child waving to his mother from the Ferris wheel at the county fair, and it is the invitation of gaudy neon in the unwashed window of a seedy strip club.

Richard Reeves, a historian and presidential biographer, credits Kennedy with realizing what few others can appreciate – 'Words matter more than deeds. You can't govern a nation with hundreds of millions of people with deeds. You can only try with words.' It is for this reason that the same words signify wildly different images and ideas to stratified and separated segments of the American populace. Donald Trump, a billionaire with expensive resorts around the world and a supermodel wife, can declare to his poor and working class white audience that he will 'make America great again,' and then hop on his private plane, sending his supporters off to their rural backyard to anticipate the reemergence of the 'good old days' over domestic beers and hand rolled cigarettes. Watching on the television at home, millions of blacks, Latinos, women, and gays view the good old days with apoplexy; images of nooses hanging from trees, the boss' hand traveling up a skirt, and police invasions of polling stations bleeding through their heads.

Barack Obama, as president, announced that he planned to enact moderate reforms to help poor people acquire medicinal treatment and health care coverage, and millions of people imagined a secret police force coercing doctors into compliance with a plan to euthanize every elderly citizen. President Obama, like Kennedy, possesses rare rhetorical and oratorical gifts, and he attempted to employ his abilities for the purposes of governance. To gain insight into he who delivers a message, it is essential to understand those on the receiving end.

Throughout American history, some presidents have represented the America to which citizens, in their most idealistic moments, aspire. Other presidents have captured the heart of darkness beating in the middle of empire – a Machiavellian machine-like organ giving life to a bloodthirsty and money hungry force of global power. Kennedy was an aspirational and inspirational force of the dream-America: the America that millions of people cheered when he visited West Berlin – half of a city he helped save from burial beneath the Iron Curtain. The America of the new frontier. The America of the moon landing. But also, the America of the Bay of Pigs.

America is at once hero and villain. JFK embodied heroic America. Nixon, his opponent in the race for the presidency, and an eventual successor, personified the villainy of the American underside. In the Oliver Stone film on the only president to resign from office, there is a scene when Anthony Hopkins, in the role of Nixon, stares at the official portrait of Kennedy and comments to himself as if he inhabits the same netherworld of the Kennedy ghost, 'When they look at you, they see what they want to be. When they look at me, they see what they are.'

The same dichotomy of fantasy versus reality played out in the juxtaposition and transition of George W. Bush to Barack Obama. Bush was largely ignorant, and he routinely debased the English language in a display of pride in his lack of sophistication, eloquence, and knowledge. Obama is not the average politician or American. Bush allowed certain Americans to take comfort and rest easy in their deficit of education and information, while Obama confronted those very same Americans with a challenge. Elegant citizenship and leadership is possible, but it demands an investment of time, thought, energy, and effort. It is hardly a surprise that the same Americans who loved Bush, while thinking, 'he's just like me,' hate Obama, because he is nothing like them. The resentment towards Obama's excellence, especially in juxtaposition with white mediocrity, paved a perilous path for Donald Trump. Far from encouraging improvement, President Jimmy Carter put it best when explained the appeal of the absurdly inexperienced Trump: 'He tapped a waiting reservoir of inherent racism.'

The Obama-America relationship is odd, because he was a leader attempting to lead from the position of not only racial minority status, but also cultural outsider status. As the culture became increasingly anti-intellectual and vulgar, it somehow twice elected an elegant intellectual as president. Obama then had to learn how to navigate the two polarities of the American identity – the dualistic personality that could produce the world's greatest universities, and the Western world's least literate population. Obama had negotiated the distance between two Americas even as a child – white and black America, but also smart and stupid, good and bad America.

Barack Obama experienced his formative years in Hawaii – the final state to join the union and one of the default vacation settings for middle Americans hoping to escape harsh winters, boring architecture, and bland culture. It is an isolated island far detached from the center of the country. Many of its natives inhabit an interesting space of internal turmoil. Their culture is independent of the United States, yet they live within one of those states. It is precisely the same drama and dilemma that many Puerto Ricans consider during debates over Puerto Rican statehood. Life in Hawaii – to the historically naked eye – would capture the beauty and diversity of the American promise. People of backgrounds divergent from the mainstream, running like a clogged artery through the heartland, can access the individualistic opportunity and institutional protection of life, liberty, and the pursuit of happiness. The gorgeous scenery, the architecture full of character and culture, and the ocean shoreline touching the sandy beaches where palm trees swing and sway to hula music, along with the sensual rhythms of the native girls would signify to any young man the limitless and boundless possibility for his own future, and the future of the nation where he will enter adulthood. Just as despair often lurked inside Obama's heart, as he missed his father and searched to gain access to a comprehensible history to inform his own biography, a heart of darkness beats within the Hawaiian breast.

In 1893, the Hawaiian monarchy, and indigenous system of government, was overthrown in an American-led coup d'état. The 'American Committee for Safety,' with a name too bizarre for Orwell, overthrew the government, and replaced it with a corporate committee of American attorneys and businessmen. The US Congress, and President Clinton, issued a joint apology to Hawaii in 1993, conceding that the annexation of the island territory was unlawful and imperial.

Even as a child, Obama would have to inhabit the contradiction of American culture. He is a biracial boy in an island state with a visible indigenous culture, finding full enjoyment in freedom, and preparing to benefit immensely from the extension and enlargement of liberty, but he stands on white settler soil. The white settler took what did not belong to him, by force in an amoral display of might makes right philosophy, and claimed it as his own. The presidency of Obama became emblematic of the insecurity of the white settler in the 21st century, but the straightjacket restraining his movement was fastened tightly by the white settler hand. Hawaii is the entire story of America, where pilgrims and pioneers once confiscated territory from the indigenous population, and often resorted to genocidal tactics to secure their own claim on resources and land that never once belonged to them. President Obama's grandparents moved to paradise from Kansas, and the president will often speak proudly and fondly of the small town values of thrift, patience, and commitment he learned from the elderly influence in his childhood. His maternal grandparents were also devout Christians. It was under the same cross and banner that Americans, operating according to the theology of 'manifest destiny,' became onward Christian soldiers marching off to war in Hawaii to claim heathen territory for themselves and their Lord.

The third location of Barack Obama's childhood was Indonesia, and it was there that he could gain insight into how the rest of the world views the United States. The vantage point of an outsider looking into America is revelatory, especially considering that 64 percent of Americans do not own a passport. Far from the altruistic defender and savior of freedom – the humanitarian crusader for equality – many other nations, especially those like Indonesia with majority Muslim populations, view America as the malevolent meddler. Unlike teenagers in the Soviet Union who associated America with the Constitution and Elvis Presley, the children in Southeast Asia, Northern Africa, and the Middle East often imagine the drone hovering overhead, or remember the rifle-armed soldier outside their home.

When Barack, as a boy, lived in Indonesia, it was under the dictatorship of Suharto, who ruled over the country for 31 years with the aid of a murderous military junta. Despite tough competition, the *New York Times* indicted Suharto's regime as one of the 'most brutal and corrupt of the 20th century.' Media censorship, a politicized judiciary, unexplained disappearances of dissidents, and death squad massacres defined Suharto's suffocation of any challenge to his absolute authority.[2] Because of his hardline position against communism, the United States assisted his ascent to power, and provided him with material and moral aid and comfort throughout his three-decade reign of terror. Hostility, and even hatred, festers for America throughout much of the world, and policies in favor of oppression and opposed to freedom are largely to blame. Barack Obama, perhaps unique among all presidents, had an intimate awareness of the contradictory character of America. He understood the evils of colonialism, and shortly after reciting the oath of office, he toured the Muslim world to announce that the United States would affirm, rather than abuse, their sovereignty. As president, he would soon personify and characterize contradiction; managing to balance efforts aimed at eradicating and extending the force of American Empire.

While a young adult, Obama would study in California, New York, and eventually make his political and personal home in Chicago. Every great city of America embodies the creative and catastrophic contradictions of America's struggle between magnanimity and inequity. In the cultural capital of the world – New York City – Obama could acquire an aesthetic education of pleasure in magnificent museums. He could select his lunch from a culinary tour of the world, sit down on a bench in a beautiful park brimming with the energy of street musicians, caricature artists offering their draftsmen talent for dollars and cents, and pedestrians and tourists of every ethnicity, sexual identity, and religious ideology. He could then transition from the beautiful to the brutal in a navigation of urban decay – the hideous blight acting as a backdrop for human obliteration. Poor blacks and Latinos huddled in tenements, seemingly shut off from the waterline of the American economy; the unquenchable thirst for sustenance and renewal manifesting in drug dependency, drive-by shootings, and gangland turf wars.

Carl Sandburg christened Chicago the 'City of Big Shoulders' – an emporium of ecstasy and agony where women and children wear 'the marks of wanton hunger,' and 'gunman kill and go free to kill again,' but also where people, too tough for 'soft cities,' lift their heads, 'singing so proud to be alive,' move and fight as 'fierce as a dog with tongue lapping for action.' For his political home and headquarters, Obama landed in the heartland's biggest city – a contradictory and paradoxical palace of Midwestern modesty and capitalistic corruption. The 'Chicago way' includes the immigrant toiling twelve hours a day in his corner deli, alongside the city alderman on the pad for a nearby slumlord.

The irony inherent in any depiction of Obama as an alien to America is that he, more than any of his predecessors, had a deep experiential comprehension of the American spirit and identity. One of the most fascinating contradictions of American culture is that while its demographics diversify, and its identity multiplies, the criteria constituting a 'real American,' becomes increasingly narrow. Republican politicians, media commentators, country musicians, and pollsters too often classify the 'real American' as a white person without a college degree who attends a Christian church and lives in a small town. According to those categories, Obama is not a 'real American,' but neither are my next door neighbors – a church attending, highly educated, middle class family in a small town of Indiana who have acquired legal citizenship after migrating from their native country of Nigeria. It would surprise no one that they identify much more with Barack Obama as an American than the projection of American identity emanating from the spray-tanned face of Donald Trump. In fact, the percentage of the country that possesses all of the 'real American' identity traits accounts for a mere twenty percent.[3] The future of America will more closely resemble the Obama family than the Bush dynasty. Political polarization pretty much traces the line of division between people who find such a prospect terrifying and those who take comfort in it.

It remains a mystery how much of his knowledge and intimacy with all the segments of the United States he infused into his oratory and policy. One always gets the sense, when observing Obama, that he is holding back a crucial part of himself. Unlike the narrator in *Invisible Man*, he does not reveal himself to those who will reject him. Rather, he locks away the edges of his potential, and the full truth of his imagination. It is likely that only his wife is aware of his spiritual safe's combination. Americans could never see Obama with clarity and rationality, and if the president would cooperate with his onlookers' obstructed vision, it was for reasons of political expedience and personal protection.

Most presidents, regardless of politics, have an intuitive understanding of the American people. It is their populist intuition that enables them to achieve their highest ambition. George W. Bush, having acclimated himself to American life in the beer halls, oil rigs, and ranches of Texas, could communicate effectively with the obtuse, but aggressive cowboy within the American heart. Growing up in an Arkansas backwater with the politically generous name of 'Hope,' Bill Clinton could reach into his memory closet to pull out the folkloric dialect familiar to Americans looking for a leader who has not strayed too far from the farm. These men could reveal themselves, slowly and steadily or in one decisive moment, and fall back on the cushion that is the fundament of their own American experience. Barack Obama did not have that comfort. He is a cosmopolitan, who would appear 'exotic' or odd, to a nation increasingly uninterested and isolated from the rest of the world. To operate at one hundred percent, making creative use of the full breadth and depth of his education and eloquence, would likely frighten most Americans, who ever since Reagan smiled at them with the grin of the corner barber, have wanted to maintain the illusion that, because they are just like the president, they too could pull the levers of power in the White House. In the words of Norman Mailer, Reagan was 'shallow as spit on a rock,' but 'smooth as a chocolate shake.'

So, Barack Obama played the character of Barack Obama – transforming his biography into allegory. 'America is good,' he assured the American people, 'because it empowers people like me – the minorities, the outsiders – to do good things.' It was a brilliant rhetorical tactic of testimony and persuasion, because it genuinely communicated pride and empowerment to non-white, non-Christian, and immigrant Americans, who could see themselves in their president, but it also slyly told white Americans, 'You can redeem yourself if you support me, and encourage people like me.' The problem, as any Catholic priest could explain, is that redemption does not appeal to those who believe they are without sin. Absolution is only possible after confession.

Those who criticize Barack Obama for having an aloof detachment from the American people are only partially correct. He is undeniably passionate about America. According to appearances, he is more passionate in his patriotism than his critics who accuse him of lacking national pride. A rhetorical question should settle that score: Who makes a better spokesman for the United States – Barack Obama or Donald Trump?

The truth of the American division is that the country never ended its civil war. In the nineteenth century, the confederacy went to war with the union over slavery, the conflict between agrarian feudalism and industrialism, and states' autonomy versus federal power. Abraham Lincoln announced the end of the physical fight in Gettysburg, but the spiritual combat never ended. In certain moments of the nation's beautiful and brutal history, the fight is easy to see – the late 1960s full of protest movements, riots, and police assaults on democracy, and the current moment on the continuum.

The election of Barack Obama signaled a triumph of the poetic America – the America of diversity and opportunity, the America of growth and expansion, the America with an open mind for evolutionary adjustment, and the America of continual hospitality where different people, new people, are always welcome to not only reside, but contribute and influence. The election of Donald Trump was an attack on that America, and an advancement of the America overly sentimental about its own power – the America obsessed with its own greatness, but transparently insecure about itself. It is that America that conquers what it desires, like Hawaii, or imposes its will with the help of strongmen on defenseless peasants, like in Indonesia. It is the America of racial caste, and systemic abuse of the unmoneyed and unconnected. Obama's patriotism had nuance, because it acknowledged the reality of two Americas in collision. Many Americans could not handle such complexity, and ran into the arms of an authoritarian whose only critique of the country was that it had become too hospitable and not sufficiently domineering. Obama loved the idea of a 'more perfect union,' but millions of its citizens could not access that love, because they themselves could not share it.

Despite his outward expression of avidity for the 'American dream' and for 'position-paper liberalism,' there is a distance between Obama and his constituents. Not only would he suffer political damage should he speak with all of the nuance and complexity of which the author of *Dreams from My Father* is clearly capable, but he would, perhaps, also absorb a psychological blow. It is the impact of a collision he would seem to suffer from surrender. So, like the invisible protagonist of Ellison's invention, he only truly gives himself away when under the full illumination of his private world.

THE SOUTHSIDE

It is hard for those privileged with the love and presence of two parents to fully understand those who suffer the abandonment of a father or mother's voluntary absence. Barack Obama writes with the melancholic notes of nostalgia about a two-week flash in his childhood when the world seemed right. His father, visiting from Kenya, lived underneath the same roof. For fourteen days, they talked into the early hours of the morning, played basketball at a nearby hoop, and formed the foundation of a bond. The foundation would eventually sink into the dirt, becoming an aborted memory of what might have been. Barack Obama's father left Hawaii, returned to Africa, and never spoke with his son again.

The friends I have made who have endured parental alienation carry a burden too big for even those who love them to contemplate. A world without a loving parent is inaccessible and inhabitable for those fortunate enough to have both guardians committed to their protection and development. Those whose mother or father reject them are more likely to practice nearly every pathology: alcoholism and drug abuse, criminality, academic failure, and in the most painful of ironies, the abandonment of their own children. The children who, as adults, weather the storm – deflecting the debris and running through the rain – must create a coping mechanism sufficient for the creation of successful, healthy, and happy lives. Anyone who has met someone whose father or mother left them, without coercion, as children will observe in the abandoned an uncanny ability to detach from immediate surroundings, and expertly compartmentalize emotions from ideas and actions. Because it is impossible to see inside them, it is unclear whether or not they are in complete control of their emotions – a command crafted to avoid the overflow of sadness and anger they must have experienced as children – or if years of pain suppression have muted and dulled the emotional life so that all but the most traumatic and dramatic fails to elicit a response.[1]

Admirers of Barack Obama often credit him for his display of enlightened detachment in the manifestation of an unbreakable cool. Republican lawmakers and leeches hurled at him invective straight out of the sewer and he barely budged. Journalists from Fox News routinely interrupted him during interviews, or asked him condescending questions, and all he offered was an exasperated tone of borderline humour. It was almost as if he was so tired of dealing with odd and irrational argumentation that he could only smirk and shrug, as he attempted, yet again, to explain something that is clear to anyone willing to invest even minimal thought into the discussion. His calm demeanor stood in stark contract to his two closest predecessors. Bush would regularly insult reporters, express dislike of media commentators, and raise his voice during debates. 'I feel your pain' became a cliché of the Clinton years, given how easily and frequently he cried. Like Bush, he would also react with rage when reporters challenged him on perceived ethical violations or inefficiencies of his administration. Obama's detractors depict his stoic poise as an aloof disregard for the suffering of Americans, and haughtiness directed toward legitimate concerns surrounding the efficacy of his policies.

Difference in partisan interpretation of Obama's personality is actually one of the few reasonable debates that exist about the Obama presidency. While most disputes involve supporters, or at least, sympathizers struggling to defend the president against the wild, baseless, and bizarre accusations of the delusional right wing fringe, the disagreement over how best to analyze Obama's stoicism has its origin in an observable fact. Barack Obama is calm, cool, and collected. Is his calm demeanor a sign of rational deliberation and impulse control, or is it the outward expression of coldhearted snobbery and hubris?

To complicate matters, black Americans are typically known for having greater comfort and creativity in the expression of their emotions than white Americans. Some critics reacted to Obama's lack of theatrical expression, along with his unique upbringing apart from traditional black neighborhoods, as reason to question his 'authenticity' and 'blackness.' Cornel West, for example, has routinely implied that Obama is not authentically black, drawing the distinction between 'racial blackness' and 'cultural blackness.' Soul and pop singer Daryl Hall, according to West, is more culturally black than Obama, because he grew up in a black neighborhood of Philadelphia and remains under the influence of the black club and church music he enjoyed and learned as a teenager. Obama, whose first full time job was as an organizer on the Southside of Chicago and who has married a black woman, and raised two black daughters, reacted with anger to West's interrogation of his ethnic loyalty. According to Michael Eric Dyson, Obama, in a thinly veiled reference to West, told a group of black intellectuals that to question his politics is legitimate, but to question his blackness is unforgivable. It was a rare display of anger from Obama, and it is revealing that it happened as a result of suspicion about his history and identity. Few things define and dictate the development of our history and identity more than family. For West, and others, to call Obama's blackness into question is to posit that he is illegitimate, because of his white mother. It insults his mother, and it insults him. In a reversal of the right wing tactic of inspection, which demonizes based on his African father, black critics of Obama's blackness make his mother's genetic influence their target, and in doing so, also insult his daughters, who share his white ancestry.

The family is what typically makes an indentation in Obama's cool exterior. It is family that first created the wound Obama might aspire to hide from the world in the development of a detached pose, and it is family that helps to heal the wound. Anything close to this subject brings out rare expressions of emotion from Obama, because it scratches at the wound.

Psychologists believe that one of the behavioral consequences to manifest in adults who suffered parental rejection as children is an aversion to intimacy. Solitude acts as a shield against the potential of repetition. Fearful of more abandonment, the adult reverts to the mind of the child seeking safety and disconnects from possible friends, lovers, and partners. Barack Obama's description of his late adolescence and early adult years conforms to psychological convention. By his own admission, he withdrew from those around him often, as during his sister and mother's visit to New York, and attempted to subtly sabotage the bonds he already enjoyed. Given that in his early years, Obama concealed himself in a sanctuary of academic study, intellectual rigor, and detached theory, it becomes significant that, for his first full time job, he entered a profession that requires regular interaction with other people, and even more so, demands that the interaction is affectionate. It is almost as if Obama's two psychological halves were in combat, and the decision to work as a community organizer issued a devastating blow to the unsocial and cynical half. Politically and personally, acting to rally the residents of poor, Chicago neighborhoods changed Obama's life. It also seems far from coincidental that the precincts where Obama lived and labored were afflicted by an epidemic of fatherless homes. By stepping into a world of absentee fatherhood, he could revisit the most confusing moments of his youth, but now with the wisdom and heart of an adult, assert himself as a positive force, rather than surrender to the status of passive victim. One woman recalled Obama acting as a mentor to her fatherless son, identifying an interest that the boy had in boats and naval ships, and often bringing toys, books, and posters related to the subject. That boy, as a young man, would eventually enlist in the Navy. The generosity, support, and encouragement that he never received from his own father he obtained, in a small way, from Obama, who still showed the bruise left by the absence of his dad.

In 2014, Obama traveled in the circular motion of reunion and homecoming. To little fanfare, he announced a new White House Initiative – My Brother's Keeper. In order to make the announcement, the president returned to the Southside of Chicago, and spoke from the auditorium of a high school with a high dropout rate where children grow accustomed to the catastrophes of urban decay: drive by shootings, drug addiction, and deprivation.

'I didn't have a dad in the house,' Obama explained, 'and

I was angry about it, even though I didn't necessarily realize it at the time. I made bad choices. I got high without always thinking about the harm that it could do. I didn't always take school as seriously as I should have. I made excuses. Sometimes I sold myself short.' In providing the power of affirmation to the young men in attendance, many also angry, the first black president told black boys that there is no limit on their potential or ceiling to their ambition. To rescue the sentiment from the cliché, he again relied on his own biography, but he also introduced new policy. The president would allocate $120 million to recruit mentors and partner them with boys who are at risk of illiteracy, educational failure, or delinquency. In the few years since its establishment, My Brother's Keeper has paired hundreds of thousands of teenagers and pre-teens with mentors, opened laboratory programs of academic assistance in inner cities throughout the country, created a Pell Grant Program for rehabilitated ex-cons who are accepted into college, and collaborated with major corporations and non-profit organizations to further the aim of mentorship, student achievement, and family stability in poor pockets of urban America. My Brother's Keeper is an example of the presidential personality in action. The motivation for the program is undeniably deeply rooted in Obama's own story. Through the modest, but profound, political policy, he attempted to prevent young boys from becoming the man he could have been had he made a few wrong turns, and help them become the man standing behind the presidential seal.[3]

Like his 2004 address to the Democratic Convention and like his famous speech on race during the 2008 election to introduce My Brother's Keeper, Obama relied on the rhetorical trick of the black preacher. The most powerful black ministers offer a testimony to underscore their theology. They present their own story as indisputable evidence of the transformative power of their faith. When Obama makes an important argument about America, he too gives testimony as foundation. The evidence of his own life is the proof of the power in 'Yes We Can.' My Brother's Keeper is affirmative of his transformation, but it is also aspirational. It is a policy of faith in family, faith in America, and faith in the possibility of continual transformation from boys like him into men like him.

My Brother's Keeper, perhaps the policy emanating most out of the president's humanity, attracted little attention from the press or pundits of any ideology. Media and public neglect of My Brother's Keeper is yet another manifestation of Obama's invisibility. Conservatives with a proclivity for stating the obvious, and in turn rejecting the structural origins and solutions to poverty, should applaud Obama for making significant moves to address the crisis of absent fathers in the inner cities. Obama's emphasis on mentorship and 'personal responsibility,' to use the most electric of all right wing buzz terms, undermines the slanderous campaign to distort the Obama image into a villainous force for Marxism and a monstrous avatar of bureaucratic ineptitude. So, the right wing has no choice but to ignore it. My Brother's Keeper functions in collaboration with 'Promise Zone' initiatives to enhance and advance public transportation in dangerous ghettos, public schools in poor pockets of major cities, and job training programs in barren territory untouched by economic recovery – all of which should give silent liberals reasons to celebrate. Such celebration would contradict the confused talking points of leftists who seek to proliferate the propaganda that Obama is a corporate sycophant disguised in a liberal mask, and that America, in all areas and all ways, is in a state of perpetual decline, largely because a dysfunctional and corrupt federal government demonstrates callous disregard for all social ills. It would also undress the popular talking point on the black left that Obama has 'done nothing for black people.' The approach that the Obama administration took to extinguishing a few of the fires that burn out hope in poverty-stricken, crime-ridden neighborhoods combined conservative philosophy with liberal intervention to showcase the potential of activist government, but because both political tribes continued to perform the ritual of blinding themselves whenever facing an encounter with the first black president, it is almost as if My Brother's Keeper, according to public perception, does not exist.

The power of Obama's own trajectory from disaffected, mischievous, and often delinquent youth to ambitious and optimistic overachiever also led him to embrace the power of forgiveness as energy source to animate public policy. As the first president to visit a federal prison and sit down with prisoners, he shared his own story, relaying how with a just a few easy to imagine different decisions, he could have found himself in a nearby cell, rather than in the Oval Office. The prison sit down session was the symbolic tip off to the most significant sea change in pardon, commutation, and criminal justice policy in the modern presidency. Obama pardoned or commuted the sentences of over 1600 nonviolent drug offenders – the most in American history. Such a groundbreaking maneuver and aggressive use of presidential power not only allows for the reintegration into society on the part of the direct beneficiaries, but it also helps to advance the movement against mass incarceration in the United States.

In the summer of 2016, the Chicago murder rate hit a 20-year high. Barack Obama, unlike on the issue of escalating imprisonment of nonviolent offenders, did not visit the city nor did he use the authority of the bully pulpit to attract attention to the gang war zone. Jesse Jackson advocates a 'White House convention on urban reconstruction' to address both the immediate catastrophe of widespread wreckage and violence, but also the longer running and long term crises of infrastructural decay, economic decline, and academic disaster placing isolated areas of Chicago, Detroit, Baltimore, and other cities into a pallid prison of imprisonment and premature death. As a former community organizer in such an undercover corner of America, Obama occupied a unique position to administer justice and restitution in cities, but instead settled for a strong, but insufficient program with coordinates of connection tracing back to his own childhood. It is a brilliant idea and wonderful program, but also something that is largely unnecessary in middle class suburbs. Willingness to scratch at the surface of problems, but refusal to explore the stratification that exists underneath is a problem with the entirety of American politics, and it is why even the most strident leftists raise legitimate arguments when they protest against incremental and gradual reform. Even with mentors, inner city children have to attend disgraceful schools, live in violent neighborhoods, and struggle against the commercial death of calcified poverty.

In Obama's urban policy, and in the absence of a more robust and ambitious agenda, Americans observed the presidential personality at its most active-positive, as he worked to partner young, lonely, and misguided men with mentors equipped to help them succeed. Equally visible, to those willing to look, was an act of presidential dissociation. The half measure is seemingly the compromise of Obama's two psychological halves – the one belonging to Obama as organizer, and the other embedded in Obama the academic.

Obama's dual halves were clearly in a duel when he accepted a position as summer associate at a corporate law firm in Chicago, while on summer break from legal classes at Harvard. It is there that he met his wife, Michelle, who, as a junior associate, was Obama's professional advisor. The first date of the eventual first couple receives graceful and sensual depiction in the film, *Southside with You*. Writer-director Richard Tanne's movie is an expression of authentic joy – the joy of romantic chemistry, the joy of fulfilled sexual desire, the joy of burgeoning love, and the joy of intimacy informed by history. The audience not only watches an energetic and erotic first date, but also becomes privy to a date with destiny, knowing that which is never referenced in the film – Barack and Michelle, the two young lawyers who have taken a liking to each other will soon become the first black family to live in the White House. One of the most compelling scenes of the movie takes place at an Afrocentric art exhibit in the Chicago Cultural Center. Barack and Michelle brilliantly analyze and emote in reaction to the paintings, paying particular attention to the beautiful depiction of ghetto nightlife in the work of Ernie Barnes. The sharp dialogue on Afrocentric visual art, along with much of the entire movie, acts as a celebration of black culture and intellectual life, giving another showcase of the cultural empowerment and advancement Obama, by proxy, helped activate and accentuate for African Americans. By becoming the most mainstream public figure in the country,

Obama, with or without intention, helped to channel black life into the mainstream of America's cultural tributary.

The film also succeeds in its depiction of the interior turmoil and tumult that inflicted Obama over the lifelong absence, and early death, of his father. Michelle detects the rage in Obama's tone and words whenever she broaches the subject, and at one point in the film, she tells him that in order to make emotional progress into the full promise of his personality and character, he must remove the weight of resentment from his shoulders. During a drive to a community meeting where Obama is scheduled to speak, the date almost derails as he all but accuses Michelle of hypocrisy; condescending to lecture her about the dubious ethics of working for a corporate law firm while she claims to have a passion for poverty relief and women's equality. Tension and silence ensue when she culminates her indictment of his judgmental arrogance with a reminder that he now works at the same firm. The hostile exchange comes late in the date when it has become clear that Barack and Michelle are beginning to form a connection. As they approach intimacy, Barack feels the self-protective need to proceed with caution, and to find the means to establish distance between him and his potential new partner and lover. He projects onto her the same flaws he would forever associate with his father: lack of commitment, self-interest at the expense of others, and an inability or unwillingness to finish what one has started. It is a classic exhibition of the psychological defense mechanism of those who have suffered the scorn of abandonment once before refusing to make themselves vulnerable to face rejection again. The problem, of course, is that all meaningful relationships require vulnerability. Intimacy is impossible without investment.[4]

Far from following in the footsteps of his father, Obama appears to have invested most thoroughly and consistently in his own family, helping to create a unit almost separate from politics. Only the right wing attempted to politicize the first family, as like the Obama administration, the Obamas were free of scandal. When Obama announced that the family would remain in Washington D.C. after his departure from the White House so as not to disrupt the high school years of their youngest daughter, it was a mere continuation of commitment to familial stability. Michelle Obama's main cause as First Lady was to advocate for more exercise and healthier cafeteria lunches in public schools. Rising to previously unknown heights of hilarity, the right wing interpreted this program as a diabolical attempt at 'social engineering,' aimed at undermining personal liberty and local autonomy. The United States has the highest childhood obesity rate in the world, which, unlike the First Lady encouraging cafeterias to stock fruits and vegetables, garners little interest from conservative defenders of 'family values.'[5]

Another boil on the body of the right is that the values of the Obama family seem pristine in comparison to most other political families, and even many American families. The cliché is that black people in American institutions have to work twice as hard to receive the same rewards as white counterparts. The Obama family has demonstrated that double might still prove insufficient. Michelle Obama, as First Lady, was central to the familial strength and stability of the Obamas, but she was also essential to the Obama presidency. In an interview on Jackie Robinson, Michelle Obama, with her husband sharing the same couch as her, argues that deserving of great praise is Jackie's spouse, Rachel Robinson.

City Lit Books

2523 North Kedzie Boulevard
773-235-2523
Chicago, IL 60647
www.citylitbooks.com

Cust: **None**

06-Sep-17 7:47p Clerk: Admin
Trns. #: 20067122 Reg: 1

9781911335306	***Barack Obama: Invisi***		
1 @ $21.99		$21.99	T
9781911335306	***Barack Obama: Invisi***		
1 @ $21.99		$21.99	T
804800040231	***Bag Tax***		
1 @ $0.07		$0.07	*
	Sub-total:	$44.05	
	Tax Tax @ 10.250%:	$4.50	
	Total:	**$48.55**	

* *Non-Tax Items*
Items: 3 *Units: 3*

Payment Via:

VISA/MC/Discover $48.55

VISA ************8126
Approval: 09522D
TroutD: 5531

Returns for store credit only, with receipt within 30 days of purchase. We cannot give credit for damaged items. Thanks for shopping local at City Lit!
See you soon!

She explains that a strong but tender woman can help center a man with great ambition. At that moment, Barack Obama removes his gaze from his wife, and smiles, with the pleasure of a child, into the camera. The absence of a parent often makes the rejected feel unworthy. To earn the affection and admiration of a woman as beautiful and brilliant as Michelle Obama could not close the canyon within Obama's spirit, but it could certainly cause it to shrink. It could have been healthy for America to aspire to a family in the White House that is closely connected, parents who seem present and adoring, and a man and woman who seem sexual. Unlike with the Clintons, living with the blemish of Bill's sex scandals, and the Bushes, one could easily imagine Barack and Michelle Obama enjoying each other in private moments of sensuality and intimacy. The confidence that Barack would build from such an experience is visible when he so easily deflects right wing ridicule, but Americans, too often disconnected from one another and sexually insecure, could not allow themselves to benefit from the example of such a couple in the White House. Black Americans, who often feature photographs of the Obamas in more tender moments in black publications, seem to understand the efficacy, while most white Americans fall into the familiar trap of ignoring, discarding, or degrading that which they cannot claim as their own. The private side of Obama might actually take comfort in the fact that his personal life, no matter the reason, is not the subject of scrutiny.

Obama's two halves seem to have negotiated an arrangement in which one remains dormant in his public life, while the other dominates his private life. Emotional attachment is rare from the presidential Obama, but seemingly ordinary for the personal Obama. The wounds of fatherly abandonment helped Obama construct armor against the silliness, but also severity, of right wing attacks on his citizenship, character, competence, and human core. Detachment turned into stoicism, allowing him to remain steady against the whirlwind of hatred and hostility. What destroyed, or at least damaged, lesser men and presidents, such as Richard Nixon and Bill Clinton, could not faze Barack Obama. There are rare moments where these two halves meet on public stage, placing a cohesive whole underneath the international spotlight.

'The hardest day' of the Obama presidency, according to the president himself, was December 14, 2012. On that fatal and fateful day, Adam Lanza, a mentally disturbed gunman, broke into the Sandy Hook Elementary School in Newtown, Connecticut and shot twenty children and six staff members. All of the victims died before the killer turned the gun on himself. The deliberate and arbitrary murder of children was an unimaginable act of evil and an unthinkable violation of every instinct necessary for the continual construction of civilization. Such an assault on human life performed a synthesis between the public Obama, who had to address the atrocity as resolute leader, and the private Obama, whose human sense of paternal love could do nothing but produce an outpouring of empathy and sensitivity.

'There isn't a parent today who doesn't feel what I do: overwhelming grief,' Obama informed the press on the day of the shooting. He began to cry, paused, and then added, 'The children had their entire lives ahead of them: birthdays, graduations, weddings.' He continued to fight tears. Then, he reflected on how he and Michelle would hug their children that night knowing that 'there are families in Connecticut who cannot do that.'[6]

Not long after the tragic afternoon of the Newtown massacre, President Obama appeared with the parents of the victims to issue a demand for greater gun control measures in the United States. With tears running from his eyes, he declared, 'Every time I think about those kids, it makes me mad, and by the way, it happens on the streets of Chicago every week.' The gun control legislation failed, giving a painful demonstration of American political dysfunction, and the madness of America's gun culture. How does a citizen react to the realization that the president, in the wake of atrocity, has displayed more aggressive humanity than the Congress with which he collaborates, and the people who he leads?

One tactic is to deny that he is human at all. That which threatened his sense of family provoked an outpouring of emotion from Obama. The emotive expression came after years of ridicule for his detachment. His critics, proving that they have no bottom but inhabit an abyss of intellectual depravity, questioned the sincerity of his sympathy. Several Fox News hosts made boring jokes about onions underneath the podium, wondered whether he was auditioning for a post-presidential career in Hollywood, and helped circulate Internet memes declaring that his tears were 'fake.'

The most crucial element of invisibility, to those who refuse to see, is its permanence. Should the invisible man suddenly become visible, the observer is confronted with a critical choice: Will he affirm the humanity he sees, and in the process, gain ugly insight into his own prejudice, hatred, and insecurity, or will he grasp at anything within proximity to cover his eyes?

Blindness becomes essential for spiritual survival.

THE MONSTER

During my first conversation with Jesse Jackson, I asked him why elements of the American right maintain a crazed hatred for him so strong that they can hardly mention his name without foaming at the mouth. Jackson leaned back in his chair, glanced out the window of his large, but surprisingly modest office, and slowly scratched his chin. 'In my most quiet moments, I often think about that,' he confessed, 'and I think that our impact was traumatizing for them. Many of them thought that when they finally got rid of King in '68, and we floundered because we were so disoriented, that they were through with us on the national level.'

Jackson is, of course, referring to an organized coalition of black politicians and activists agitating for freedom, opportunity, and justice when he uses the pronoun 'us.' In the 1970s, Jackson became what one historian calls an 'apostle of economics,' fighting racially corrupt businesses and trade unions that were unwilling to hire or admit black workers. The campaign that he led could claim as victory tens of thousands of jobs for black Americans, along with the ethnic integration of organized labor. In the next decade, Jackson ran for president twice, nearly capturing the Democratic nomination on the latter run, and in doing so, he galvanized and energized a new class of black political leadership. Out of his campaign came the election of the first black governor of Virginia, the first black mayors of Memphis, Denver, Los Angeles, and New York, and large numbers of black congressmen and women. The Jackson candidacy also convinced the Democratic Party to move to a proportional allocation of delegates in their primary system. The winner-take-all system that preceded proportionality produced results like in 1984 when Jackson won twenty-one percent of the popular vote, but received only three percent of the delegates. Proportionality empowered Obama to win in 2008. Given that his primary opponent, Hillary Clinton, won New York, California, Texas, Ohio, and Florida, she surely would have secured the nomination, and Obama would have never become president without proportional delegation. Economic empowerment of black Americans, the diversification of American government, and the democratization of the Democratic Party are all achievements on the Jackson resume. White authority and supremacy withstood Jackson's assault with the solidity of a screen door matched against Muhammad Ali's fists. It is for these reasons, and many more, that Obama owes much of his own success to the pioneer propulsion of Jesse Jackson. Before Obama could win the presidency, Jackson had to run for the presidency, and before Obama became the right wing's greatest villain – a monster of apocalyptic threat – Jackson was also on the receiving end of hysterical vilification.

There exists a long and sad tradition in American politics of paranoid delusion and fear. Although the hard left is occasionally guilty of seeing demons lurk in every shadow, the right wing has consistently exercised the most extreme form of substituting hallucination for political interpretation. The John Birch Society, a far right extremist group, believed that President Dwight D. Eisenhower, a former Army General, was a secret agent for the Communist Party receiving marching orders from the Kremlin, and many conservatives would imagine far worse of Eisenhower's successor, John F. Kennedy.[1] The Clinton family has faced accusations of everything from drug smuggling to premeditated murder.[2] No one, however, has made an entire bloc of voters in American politics collectively lose their minds and slip into delirium like Barack Obama. The element of race makes paranoia much more combustible. As historian Carol Anderson explains, 'The trigger for white rage is black advancement. White rage punishes black resilience and black resolve.' Who is a more effective and transformative symbol of black advancement, and therefore much likelier to cause mass hallucination, than Barack Obama?

Ellison's narrator – the invisible man – writes that among the masses that cannot see him, there is a sizable group that views him as the 'figure in a nightmare.' Because he is the phantom who haunts their nights, they dream of his destruction. For eight years, the right wing gazed, with a gap-mouthed stare, upon the president from this absurd vantage point. There is no rational explanation for the fear and hostility that the hard right, including Senators and members of Congress, display toward Obama. It is simply a reaction to trauma. If Jesse Jackson's psychoanalysis of his enemies is correct, it is exponentially truer for Obama. Jackson, among many others, caused structural damage in the fortress of white supremacy and authority. Obama was the first, and only, person to storm the castle and seize the throne.

Millions of Americans who see the black man as a threat, and by extension view the black president as a walking and talking nuclear weapon, demonstrated a dexterous imagination when considering what Obama was really planning and enacting behind closed doors in the White House.

Noam Chomsky, linguist and political philosopher, has often identified 'white fear of revenge' as a manipulative emotional force in American culture and politics.[3] On a subconscious level, many whites might feel afraid that eventually blacks are going to try to even the score of oppression for all of the years they suffered under slavery and segregation. Such paranoid delusion is responsible for Rush Limbaugh's claim that 'in Obama's America, the white kids now get beat up with the black kids cheering,' Republican congressman Steve King's assertion that Obama 'has a default mechanism that favors the black person,' and thousands of Tea Party activists charging Obama with support for 'white slavery.'[4]

Whatever strange and twisted form of psychology is at work, there clearly is not a reasonable ideology behind the beliefs of conspiracy theorists who transformed Obama into the devil – a mysterious and omnipresent force responsible for all evil. A large number of Republicans believe that Obama is an illegal immigrant born in Kenya, secretly smuggled through customs by his Marxist mother (51 percent), a closeted Muslim who sympathizes with terrorist organizations such as the Muslim Brotherhood and ISIS (43 percent), and that he received training to engineer a radical overthrow of the US government.[5] According to Public Policy Polling, one of the most respected opinion research firms in the United States, 13 percent of Republicans believe that Obama is the 'antichrist,' while another 13 percent are 'not sure' – apparently, still reviewing the evidence.[6] Because the American media insists on treating the American people like children, the alarming data on the insipid and insidious beliefs of Republican voters rarely enters the discussion. When Hillary Clinton described the beliefs of most Trump supporters as 'deplorable,' commentators roundly rebuked her, rather than investigate the claim. Even a cursory glance at the evidence would confirm that at least half of Trump voters had bigoted views, and harbored illusions that Obama, in collaboration with the same people who brought down the Twin Towers, was personally committed to their annihilation.

It is hard to imagine what it is like to live as these people. You wake up in Pittsburgh or South Bend, and you think, 'Well, it's another day. The President is an illegal immigrant plotting to give the country over to terrorists who will bring us closer to Armageddon.' Then, you still have to drop your children off at school and pick up groceries for dinner. While you are in the checkout line, all of this madness is raging inside your skull. It might become therapeutic for some of the more deeply disordered, but it is far from harmless.

At all levels, the belief that Obama is a subversive agent of darkness infects the host with the severity of arsenic. At the highest floor of governance, it paralyzed the possibility of bipartisan progress. Republican Senate leader Mitch McConnell infamously announced shortly after the first electoral victory of Barack Obama that his top priority and number one goal was to ensure that Obama was a 'one term president.' McConnell represents and resides in a state with the poorest county in the country. The declaration of focus not on poverty reduction, literacy, or educational mobility, but the defeat of the president, and the refusal to negotiate with his agenda, acted as an honest prelude to the unprecedented obstruction Obama would face as chief executive. For the first time in the nation's history, Congress refused to hold hearings for a president's nomination to the Supreme Court. They refused to simply meet with the judge, even though his qualifications are impeccable and his record is moderate. Republicans would not work with Obama on his health care reform plan, even though they were quick to condemn it, and subsequent to its passage, held dozens of failed votes to repeal it. The GOP also held numerous hearings to investigate Hillary Clinton's alleged, but nonexistent, criminality in a terrorist attack on the American consulate in Benghazi, Libya that took place while she was Secretary of State, but did not even consider Obama's proposals for tuition-free community college, or subsidized access to high speed broadband internet connections in unwired sections of rural America.

Conspiracy theories, throughout American history, found audience only in the far right and far left fringes of American culture. William F. Buckley, the dean of conservative intellectuals, gained significant credibility in the 1960s when he aggressively denounced the John Birch Society. The presidential campaign of 2015 and 2016 showcased an ugly mutation of the Republican Party. Apparently, the voting base had grown so extreme in their paranoia and hatred of Obama that they were willing to believe anything, so long as it had the cheap excitement of the cloak and dagger. Donald Trump not only established his bonafides with enunciation and endorsement of birtherism, but he called Obama and Hillary Clinton the 'cofounders of ISIS,' stated as if it was self-evident, that the election system is 'rigged,' and cryptically announced that Obama is 'weak on terrorism,' because there is 'something going on there.' Trump's revival tent ramblings were not liabilities for him to overcome, but moments of ingratiation toward an increasingly resentful and conspiratorial constituency. The right wing's comfort with conspiracy theory also led to the acceptance of 'fake news' –

stories of pure fabrication, with headlines like 'The Clinton Murders,' that floated around social media. The Republican Party's failure to follow the example of Buckley, and repudiate the lies and distortions of its more rabid followers, amounts to a violation of the public trust, and a willingness to spread dangerous fallacy to advance its own agenda.

Part of the right wing's irresponsible and unethical neglect of its own professional duty and of the public interest was, according to Obama, political calculation. 'If they cooperated with me, then that would validate our efforts. If they were able to maintain uniform opposition to whatever I proposed, that would send a signal to the public of gridlock, dysfunction, and that would help them win seats in the midterms.' The President elaborated that, while the tactic makes for smart politics, it is 'bad for the country.' The consequences of political detachment seemed not to bother Republican leaders. Opposition to Obama led the conservative party – a once important and often insightful part of political discourse – to mutate into a juvenile collection of paranoiacs with no interest in governance, only an obsession with prosecuting their holy war against Barack 'Lucifer' Obama.

Donald Trump presented himself as an archangel qualified to slay Satan's earthly administrator. His nomination, and eventual victory, continued the conservative resistance to governance and politics. Without any experience, and little knowledge, he was able to defeat a former Secretary of State, senator, and first lady for the presidency. His ignorance on matters as simple as 'how a bill becomes a law' never seemed to slow down his polling. Republican voters, and millions of politically unaffiliated Americans, demonstrated that political, historical, and legal awareness is not a qualification they consider important for the most powerful office in the country. Supporting the candidacy of Donald Trump was the equivalent of letting someone fly a plane who has never even sat behind the wheel of a car. A crash seems likely, but the disastrous course began during the Obama administration when Republicans signified that their only activity of interest was to disparage and despise the first black president.

Republican officials, likely suffering from the derangement of white supremacy, subjected President Obama to insult and indignity the likes of which few other public figures have ever experienced. When President Obama stepped off Air Force One in Arizona, the state's governor, Jan Brewer, did not give the typical greeting that presidents are accustomed to receiving from state administrators, regardless of party. She stormed up to him, interrupting his attempt at a 'hello,' and started lecturing him, waving her finger in his face, fulminating about the perceived inadequacies of his immigration policy. During Obama's 2009 address to Congress on the Affordable Care Act, the President experienced unprecedented disrespect, ostensibly over immigration, but anyone who is remotely perceptive understands that these displays of petulance derive from deep psychological insecurity. Obama explained that the Affordable Care Act would not provide subsidized health coverage to illegal immigrants, a demonstrable fact, and was soon interrupted by South Carolina Congressman Joe Wilson, who, looking like every belligerent drunk attempting to bully the bartender, screamed, 'You lie!' The President offered no rebuttal, or even acknowledgement of the taunt. One could credibly argue that because American presidents are not kings or queens, a little less deference, and a little more expressiveness, might well serve the culture of democracy.

Meetings of the British Parliament seem much livelier and more productive, for example, than the library-like, whispered conversations of the Senate, but the fact that the first president to receive direct disrespect is also the first black president seems like much more than a coincidence. Questions surrounding not the efficacy, but the legitimacy of Obama found amplification from Republican officials, because right wing voters lived for such moments. Those moments fueled much of Trump's campaign, because as a savvy entertainer and marketer, he understood that his audience was desperate for extreme rhetoric. He also observed the ugly lessons of the John McCain campaign. The Senator who challenged Obama for the presidency in 2008 found himself overwhelmed by unmoored voters at rallies confronting him about Obama's evil intentions, Islamic motivation, and foreign birth. Much to his credit, McCain continually denounced the personal and paranoid attacks on Obama, insisting that Obama is a 'good, family man and honorable American,' and that they just 'have many disagreements.' The audiences consistently booed McCain's defense of Obama's humanity, and eventually the right wing talk radio goblins would condemn him for it. Trump avoided making the same tactical error in his courtship of the conservative base.

At the basement levels of intelligence and populism, the rank and file Republicans behaved with the logic and manners of a mob running on fumes of laughing gas. Voters have empowered the worst elements of far right politics, culminating in the nativist, white nationalism of Donald Trump, who has advanced anti-intellectualism and ignorance to a new prominence, and brought bigotry back to the mainstream. As president, Trump empowers and enhances

American culture's most vulgar, course, and cruel elements.

I received a glimpse into the monstrous turn American politics was making, and the hideous destination that the right wing had mapped, when I covered an early Tea Party rally in Valparaiso, Indiana, a small college town, and the home of my graduate school alma mater, Valparaiso University. The Tea Party was a group of disaffected whites angry over the size of the deficit, and hostile to Obama's health care proposal. Immediately, there were troubling signs of dissonance and inconsistency. Tea Party devotees never expressed concern when their beloved President George W. Bush enlarged the deficit by exponential proportions when he, unlike every other president in American history, conducted war while cutting taxes. Signs at Tea Party functions, made without attempt at irony or humor, telling the government to 'keep their hands off Medicare,' were common eyesores. Due to evident inconsistency and hypocrisy, many critics began to form the suspicion that the Tea Party's motivational claim was fiscal conservatism, but the real inspiration was their frenzied, irrational opposition to the election of Barack Obama.

At a rally of a Tea Party organization in 2010, I met friendly but confused people who believed that Obama was an enemy of atomic force. Many of them demonstrated kind qualities that contrasted with their mean-spirited politics, but would offer comically over-the-top conjecture as evidence against the newly-elected president. 'He is taking away our freedoms,' they would announce as if it was self-evident, but struggle to identify one such liberty when I pressed for details and examples. One man unknowingly made a fool of himself when he told me, 'The government ruins everything it touches.' He was wearing a t-shirt from Yellowstone National Park. Rather than embarrass him, I merely nodded and continued taking notes. The members of the crowd seemed misguided, but benign enough until the rally's featured speaker grabbed hold of the microphone. In a nasal voice that gave amusing effect to his tough guy pose, he declared that a war was coming in America, and assured the crowd that the president was on the enemy side. He openly speculated about Obama's origin of birth, and offered a badly fabricated quote from *The Audacity of Hope* as damning proof of the president's treasonous intentions: 'If America has to go to war with radical Muslims, I'll stand with the Muslims.'

Never mind the stupidity and bigotry of referring to 1.1 billion people as 'the Muslims,' as if they were a monolith, but the actual quote from Obama's book is a defense of American-Muslims' constitutional protections of privacy, liberty, and property:

> In the wake of 9/11, my meetings with Arab and Pakistani Americans, for example, have a more urgent quality, for the stories of detentions and FBI questioning and hard stares from neighbors have shaken their sense of security and belonging. They have been reminded that the history of immigration in this country has a dark underbelly; they need specific assurances that their citizenship really means something, that America has learned the right lessons from the Japanese internments during World War II, and that I will stand with them should the political winds shift in an ugly direction.

The crowd likely did not know that their beloved speaker was either misinformed or manipulative, judging from the roaring applause and shouts of affirmation they gave him after each point. It seems just as likely they would not care if they found out. When I emailed the speaker with the correct Obama quote, giving the full citation of his book with the page number, he replied by calling me a 'dishonest coward.' He then proceeded to email me daily for the next month with a stream of boring invective not worthy of publication. The birther and conspiracy theory nonsense destroyed any faith that the Tea Party assembled to argue for fiscal solvency. Instead, as the speaker at the Valparaiso rally demonstrated, they were more interested in resurrecting the insinuations of the 2008 campaign that, because Obama had associated with 'radical' figures, he himself was a radical, whose aspirations were unworthy of trust.

Central to the McCarthy-like guilt-by-association campaign of slander was Bill Ayers, the man Sarah Palin, with characteristic eloquence, referenced when she accused Obama of 'palling around with terrorists.' The plot and ploy to make Obama appear as an enemy of the state, with a not-so-subtle manipulation of his race and Arabic name, began before Obama even moved into the White House. Ayers went from an obscure college professor to a household celebrity as soon as Palin identified him as the other party in Obama's terroristic friendship. Ayers, in actuality, was a member of the Weather Underground – an anti-Vietnam war organization – and had admitted to participating in acts of property destruction and politicized vandalism. He and associates placed a small explosive device in a Pentagon closet, the explosion of which caused the ruination of files and a leak in a pipe. Later, they would blow up a statue outside of Chicago Police Headquarters. Ayers has admitted that the bombings were reckless. If some unlucky janitor or pedestrian found themselves in the vicinity of the blast it could have resulted in severe injury, but Ayers and the Weather Underground did their best to avoid harming any human beings, and they succeeded. Not one person suffered even a bruise because of their bombings. Only in America can Bill Ayers become the public enemy in the historical memory of a war that resulted in the deaths of millions of Vietnamese people and 58,000 Americans, even after the acting Secretary of Defense at the launch of the war has admitted on public record that the pretextual justification for the invasion of Vietnam was a lie. After the war ended, Ayers earned a Ph.D. in education, and eventually became a professor at the University of Illinois in Chicago. He and Obama sat on a board together for the Woods Fund, a non-profit that awards grants to innovative projects in Chicago schools. Many right wing theorists believe that Ayers ghostwrote Obama's memoir, *Dreams from My Father*, even though they co-served at the Woods Funds three years after the book's publication. Clearly, a black candidate for president, even with his Ivy League pedigree, is incapable of writing a critically acclaimed, bestselling memoir without the assistance of a white radical.

Because Ayers is an interesting man, and because I cannot resist the opportunity to pal around with a terrorist, I sat down for coffee with him to discuss his experience in the eye of the right wing hurricane, and what it taught him about the fear and loathing of the first black president:

> Obama's self-definition was moderate, middle of the road, pragmatic politician. Those of us who knew him thought of him as all of those things, plus compassionate, decent, and smart – the smartest guy in the room no matter who else was in the room. But the

> right looked at him and saw a secret Muslim, palling around with terrorists, who has socialist tendencies, and is a hidden black nationalist. The left looked at him and said, 'I think he's winking at us.' So, when he said, 'I'm evolving on gay rights,' the left said, 'No, he agrees with us.' Well, no, he was evolving. No one took him at his word. Everyone insisted on painting their own graffiti over the Obama portrait.

It did not take much provocation for Ayers, a longtime veteran of the civil rights movement who taught in one of the first black freedom schools in Michigan, to connect the vandalism of Obama's identity with the larger experience of black misrepresentation in America. 'As a black person in America no one can see you,' he posited, 'Everyone ascribes to you all of their fears and fantasies, because they can't bear it themselves.'

There is no one more qualified to give insight into the vilification of Obama than Ayers, considering that he was made into Exhibit A in the supposed case against the first black presidential nominee of the Democratic Party. If Obama is a monster, then Ayers was Dr. Frankenstein, perfecting the ghoul in his underground laboratory. 'In the far right fever swamps,' Ayers added, 'my father paid his way to Harvard. My father was a liberal businessman who found Obama, and funded my creation of a Manchurian candidate.'

Beyond describing the layers of lunacy, Ayers offers an indictment of the narrow narrative passing for political debate in the frenzy of electoral politics:

In 2008, no one could figure out how to debate Obama, because he was so skilled, telegenic, and charismatic. So, instead of taking him on the policy stage, and actually dealing with the issues, they created a story, and the story was that no one knew anything about this young man from Illinois. He has no record, and therefore we need to be careful about this enigmatic, first term Senator from Illinois. We don't know him, but we know his friends. Who are his friends? A black nationalist preacher, a Palestinian scholar who says Israel is a rogue state, a white messianic priest who hangs out in the black ghetto, and a former terrorist. The convenience of me is that I have a history with the Weather Underground. So, I can be conveniently tarred as an unapologetic terrorist, and the unapologetic part is that I'm on the far left still. Because they could not undercut Obama's appeal, and they could not defeat him in a debate on issues, they offered guilt by association to argue that he was illegitimate. It is astonishing how well it works, and I say it works well, because a couple of days after the election I was on CNN, and Chris Cuomo kept trying to say, as they all did, and this is a liberal, was 'What is your relationship with Barack Obama?' None of them said, 'Who gives a shit?' As it went along, no one challenged the premise. They only attempted to deny the connection. The *New York Times* ran a long report concluding that we did not know each other very well. Whereas I wrote an op-ed, and the *Times* was good enough to run it, in which I argued that in a wildly diverse democracy, having contact with

> the widest range of people is not a sin, it is a virtue. I wrote that because I was angry over the fact that all the liberals did not reject the guilt-by-association tactic. They only tried to deny the association.

Barack Obama did have a connection with Ayers, he did attend the church of Jeremiah Wright – a black nationalist, he did maintain a relationship with Michael Pfleger, a radical Catholic priest on Chicago's largely black Southside, and he was friends with Edward Said, one of the most respected Palestinian scholars in the world. These are interesting people, and most of them offer valuable services to their communities. Ayers is correct in his recommended response – an oscillation between indifference and applause. Regardless, none of these friendships or working relationships suggests that Obama had nefarious or dangerous intentions. The slander and smear of Obama quickly failed to survive the scrutiny of Obama's record, and is even harder to maintain after two terms of an Obama presidency. He has championed moderate to slightly liberal reforms of the health care system, economic regulatory institutions, and social policy, but has never once validated the right wing paranoia portraying him as a radical terrorist in establishment drag. One of the most stunning turns of American politics is that, even after Obama's eight years of moderate, mainstream governance, all polling data indicates that large numbers of Republican voters continue to believe he is a subversive threat to all that is sacred; that he is a Zulu warrior hell-bent on performing abortions against the wishes of every Christian woman. Much of Trump's rise to Republican heights was predicated on the notion that Obama was an irredeemable cancer on America's body politic. Trump presented himself as the cure, and many strange and delusional white people believed him. Of course, Ayers is correct that Obama, love or loathe his policies, is right in the center of American political debate. No matter how much Obama is part of the normal and predictable liberal tradition of two-party politics, his election did strike a devastating blow to white supremacy. Ayers understands much of the off-the-scale hatred and hostility toward Obama as an attempt to psychically recover from that impact:

> Abolition and black reconstruction in the South led to the terror, reactionary governments criminalizing black life, and the rise of the Ku Klux Klan. All of those events took place in reaction to abolition. The Civil Rights Movement had the reaction of mass incarceration, the rise of the right, the Southern Strategy, and voter suppression. It is worth noting in both directions that forty percent of white people voted for Obama. On one level that seems tiny and sad, but from another angle it is really encouraging and amazing that in a country with this history, forty percent of white people voted for the black candidate against the white candidate. The Obama presidency was significant, and the reaction to it was significant. In matters of race, the reaction is always violent, hateful, and sometimes overwhelming. Obama agitated the continual conversation and tension over how and when we will fully reconcile for our racial sins.[7]

Martin Luther King, decades before the Obama victory, diagnosed white America's 'schizophrenic personality on the question of race.' Much like Ayers, King suggested that 'America is torn between two selves – a self in which she proudly professed the great principles of democracy and a self in which she sadly practiced the antithesis of democracy. This tragic duality produced a strange indecisiveness and ambivalence toward the negro, causing America to take a step backward simultaneously with every step forward on the question of racial justice.' It is impossible to deny that the election of Obama was a leap forward, but the animus that followed, and the transition to Trump amounts to that simultaneous step backward.

On election night in 2012, Barack Obama won a second term by defeating Mitt Romney, a respectable and credible candidate, and a clean-cut entrepreneur and governor who came to personify every quality about the old guard that represented and wielded American power up until just a decade ago. Right wing idol, Bill O'Reilly, with a tone of exasperation and facial expression of depression, looked as if his mother had just died when Megyn Kelly, former queen of the Fox News kingdom, asked, 'How did we get here?' O'Reilly's answer was surprisingly honest, 'It is a changing country. The demographics are changing. It is not a traditional America anymore. Twenty years ago, Obama would be roundly defeated by an establishment candidate like Mitt Romney. The white establishment is now a minority. You're going to see an overwhelming Hispanic vote for Obama, overwhelming black vote for Obama, and women are going to break for Obama. People feel that they are entitled to things, and which candidate between the two is going to give them things?'[8]

Worthy of acknowledgement is that for O'Reilly, and the massive audience that adores him, the 'establishment' should forever remain a white fraternity, and that blacks, Latinos, and women who challenge the exclusion of the establishment are not acting according to a political ideology or strong sense of citizenship, but in a selfish interest to 'get things.' The white revenge fantasy is audible in the hidden notes of such a diagnosis. Formerly persecuted minorities cannot gain power without then waging war against anyone sharing ancestry with the former persecutors. Power is a zero sum game. African Americans, Hispanics, and women will not settle for representation, opportunity, and justice. They want 'things.' Cue the ominous music.

The pathetic belief in victimhood running through conservative circles of white America, along with delusions of persecution, found relief in the violent impulse of American history; the same violent impulse Ayers identified as always intensifying after black advances in freedom, opportunity, and equality. In the eight years of the Obama presidency, the number of white supremacist, neo-Nazi, and potpourri hate groups rose from just over one hundred to nearly one thousand. Many members of racist organizations are, undoubtedly, armed and dangerous. The Obama election provoked historic levels of gun ownership throughout the United States, with the gun industry enjoying a $9 billion boost during Obama's two terms.[9] The number of armed state militias increased from 42 in 2008 to 276 in 2016.[10] Derangement and paranoia over a black presidency led to an awakening of America's undercurrent of violence, prejudice, and anti-government aggression. The nomination of Donald Trump, along with the wild rhetoric audible every night on right wing radio and television, indicates that even if extremists of bigotry constitute a minority, they are a sizable, influential, and harmful minority. This same minority is convinced that Obama is a black radical in the tradition of the Black Panther Party. Superstar right wing commentator Glenn Beck once declared that Obama 'hates white culture,' while many Republicans attack Obama, who was diplomatic to a fault, as the 'most divisive president in American history.' [11] Much to the complaint of many African American activists, Obama routinely avoided race as a target for his policy and topic of his rhetoric. Just as too many white homeowners see a black family moving to the neighborhood as a threat out to get them, white Republicans participated in 'white flight' from rational debate, and projected their own prejudices onto Obama. Some of them host radio shows, and others collect firearms and join militias. The hatred and resistance to progress that they have in common was sufficient to drive Donald Trump into the White House. Trump's candidacy and victory fall perfectly into the pattern Bill Ayers eloquently describes. He is the vicious reaction to black progress. As historian Carol Anderson understands, Trump's amplification and personification of white rage is the enactment of political 'punishment for black resilience and black resolve.'

If the mélange of hatred were not a menace, it would become easy to laugh at all the onward Christian soldiers marching off to the gun shop after church. The joke is on them, because their ideology and interpretation of history is so thoroughly divorced from reality that it can barely claim home in the same universe as the truth. President Barack Obama is far from a radical, and the reforms he did champion have consistently created better living conditions for all Americans, even those whose idea of recreation is playing G.I. Joe in empty fields on Saturday night.

When Barack Obama ran for high office in 2008, he made a campaign stop in the small town of Elkhart, Indiana. Elkhart is a charming representation of provincial America, but like many American villages and cities, it wrestles against darker demons of exclusion and fear. The financial collapse of the subprime mortgage crisis crushed Elkhart, and when Obama made his campaign stop, he received indication that its largely white population was open to support anyone who could help rescue them from the pit of privation. Their unemployment rate was at a devastating twenty percent, and local businesses were closing their doors and boarding their windows, causing the downtown commercial district to resemble a bone yard of bankruptcy. In 2016, the unemployment rate had fallen to 3 percent, and the local economy's recovery was so robust that business owners had taken to recruiting low level workers straight out of the homeless shelter in a neighboring town. Shocking and appalling both the mayor of Elkhart and the president of Elkhart's Chamber of Commerce, the residents of a great success story of Obama's America had turned against its author. To pollsters and journalists, Elkhart voters routinely expressed disdain and disgust with Obama over non-economic issues, using the inflated, and often insidious rhetoric of the Tea Party: 'He is stripping away our freedoms,' 'He isn't a true American,' etc. At a high school basketball game, the entire audience chanted 'build the wall' and 'Trump' at a visiting team with a predominantly Latino roster.[12]

Opposition to Obama never had the basis of any rational metric. It is not just the hostility towards Obama that provokes distortion of his record, which in reality is full of accomplishment, but disbelief over Obama's success, among a large group of media commentators and observant citizens, that leads to an apocalyptic depiction of America in decline. The true story is that much of the nation, contrary to alarmist reports of doom and gloom, resembles Elkhart: The general standard of living is good, but unhappy people, reticent to reflect on their own lives, project their own neuroses and frustrations onto politics. Obama was the perfect target, because just as Ayers explained, his race and seemingly 'exotic' ethnic background makes him an ideal archetype for the ascription of fears and fantasies.

Gore Vidal once rechristened America as the 'United States of Amnesia.' Like a drunk on a lifelong bender, the American polity wakes up every morning having forgotten what happened the night before. Just as Elkhart residents cannot recall that in 2008 they were begging Obama to rescue them from the misery of widespread unemployment, Americans have buried the trauma of the financial collapse in their subconscious, and have lost the ability to compare the liquidation of the mortgage crisis with the elevation of the Obama recovery. The unemployment rate is now below five percent, and under Obama, the American economy had the longest period of job growth on record. The real estate market has recovered to near pre-crash levels, while manufacturing productivity is also at a historic high.[13] For all the constant crying and carping about 'income inequality' and 'decline in wages,' the upper middle class in America is at its strongest and largest at any time on record. Thirty percent of American households generate over $100,000 dollars in annual income, and another thirty-two percent rest comfortably in the middle class. Only nineteen percent qualify as 'poor' or 'near poor,' one of the lowest levels on record since 1979.[14] In fact, during the final year of the Obama presidency, the poverty rate saw its largest drop since 1968, and 2015 showed the largest single year increase in median income, affecting all income levels, in American history. America is not an Edenic paradise, free of all struggle and strife, but it is far from the Dantean circle of Hell most commentators, especially those of the far right and hard left, describe with all the subtlety and sophistication of a street-side megaphone preacher.

With any economy as large as the United States – the largest in the world – it is impossible to attribute growth or decline to one cause or contributor, but it requires an act of faith rivaling even the most religious believer, to deny President Obama his share of praise for America's escape from depression and entrance into prosperity. Right wing pessimists attempt to have their hallucinogenic drug and ingest it too when they evaluate the performance of Obama on economic issues. When confronted with news of progress and improvement, they protest that the president has little to do with financial changes throughout the country, but in the same exasperated breath, they will also claim that the United States is experiencing the 'slowest recovery from recession on record' and that there are 'historic numbers of Americans out of the workforce.' Both of these developments are, of course, entirely the fault of Barack Obama. Reality, always stubborn, reveals a different picture. The recovery, which is quite good, is slower than other recoveries, not because of Obama, but because the recession from which it is recovering is the worst on record. The labor force participation rate is at its lowest point since the 1960s, not because Obama employed black magic to keep people out of work, but because of unprecedented numbers of baby boomers, the largest generation in American history, taking early retirement, and the historic high of 18-22 year olds enrolled in college. As has become typical in American politics, much of the debate has everything to do with histrionics and personality, and little to do with public policy.[15]

The economic stimulus package Obama championed at the onset of his presidency had strategic distribution to municipal governments so as to save millions of public sector jobs, and make possible small town and state infrastructure development projects to create jobs. Tax credits for low and middle-income households gave workers financial assistance when they needed it most, while the imposition of higher tax rates on the wealthy generated additional revenue for federal spending. Elkhart, Indiana, like many small villages and mid-sized cities, accepted stimulus money, which went to the direct improvement of the local economy. Obama's enhancement of the Bush bailouts for the banking industry remains controversial, but less contentious is the bailout policy for the auto industry.

The resuscitation of a dying automobile manufacturing hub of the American economy enabled millions of workers to retain their jobs, and allowed for the survival of thousands of businesses connected to auto parts, vehicular sales, and equipment transportation. It is worthy of acknowledgement and remembrance that the federal government has collected all of its bailout money, with interest, back from the recipients on Wall Street and in Detroit. Obama also helped ensure fairness in the application of economic policy and law with his signature on the Dodd-Frank bill – a set of regulations against the financial industry designed to prevent future crises. The bill included the creation of the Consumer Financial Protection

Bureau, a new federal agency committed to reimbursing borrowers who suffered from unscrupulous, manipulative, or exploitative practices from banks and other lending institutions. 25 million consumers have received assistance from this agency since its establishment in 2009. While far from perfect, and never able to erase distinctions in treatment that separate the wealthy from what Michael Harrington called, 'the other America,' Dodd-Frank and the CFPB does strengthen the chances of survival for a typical middle or working class citizen. A thriving middle class conflicts with the dystopian folklore of media popularity, but it is not lost with 18-35 year-olds in America, who demonstrate higher levels of hope and optimism than any other age demographic in the country.

The United States of America currently has nearly the largest amount of young people enrolled in college at any point in its history, and in my own experience as a college instructor, I see most of my former students matriculate into the fields of their own choice shortly after graduation. The data supports my anecdotal evidence. In 2015, the National Association of Colleges and Employers surveyed 244,000 Americans who graduated college with a bachelor's degree in 2014. Eighty-two percent of graduates reported a 'positive outcome' since commencement, with over sixty percent in full time, professional employment, and nearly twenty percent continuing their studies in a full time graduate degree program.[16] Contrary to the college or nothing dichotomy of financial forecast in much of the media, the trades are also quite reliable. The overwhelming majority of people who earn certification in welding, for example, secure full time, salaried employment within one year. A major accelerant of young Americans' ride into economic stability and financial success, regardless of educational background or career aspiration, is the Affordable Care Act, President Obama's signature achievement.

Predictions surrounding the passage of 'Obamacare,' at time of broadcast and even more so in retrospect, resemble recordings from the psychiatric unit of a county hospital. Like the opening notes of the heavy metal classic from Venom, right wing analysts thundered, 'Welcome to hell!' as Obama signed the ACA into law. The sweeping health care reform legislation would cause massive layoffs, bankrupt Medicare, and create a cruel rationing system against the elderly, leaving senior citizens in pain and out of options. The irony infused into the hysteria surrounding the ACA is that the program has conservative philosophical roots, and a Republican precedent for enforcement. The right wing Heritage Foundation, dating back to the 1980s, proposed a governmental mandate on each citizen to purchase health insurance, while Republican nominee for president in 1996, Bob Dole, campaigned on a reform plan strikingly similar. On the state level, it was actually Barack Obama's 2012 opponent, the moderate Mitt Romney, who implemented the exact same system while governor of Massachusetts. The fiercest and fairest criticism a rational observer could lay against the program is that it is too cautious and conservative. Obama should have, at least, attempted to better balance market control over medicine with governmental regulation and supervision. The President's original proposal included a 'public option' to compete with private plans. The public option would have extended Medicare to all citizens, regardless of age, and fully ushered America into the 21st century by offering health care as a right for all, rather than an expensive service affordable to the few. Considering that the Affordable Care Act passed the Senate by a mere eight votes, and that subsequent to its passage the Republican Party has demonstrated an obsession with repealing the law, even going so far as to challenge the mandate at the Supreme Court, Obama's removal of the most controversial element might amount to shrewd and savvy political strategy. The tactical and moral dilemma between bold ambition and pragmatic calculation complicates every aspirational presidency, and it was a conflict at the core of the Obama agenda. No one reasonable, not even an Obama partisan, could argue that the Affordable Care Act is without flaw, but the leftist, academic theoretician approach to analysis screams of a detachment so severe it disqualifies the critic from conversation. If the left wing professor or pundit argues that Obama failed, because his reform is not sufficiently transformative, one need only identify the millions of people whose lives have immeasurably improved because of the bill to offer a swift slap down. If the argument for perfection, divorced from reality, continues unabated, it is a significant signal that the arguer is not a serious person.

There is no doubt that any reform as substantial as the Affordable Care Act is worthy of criticism and subject to improvement, but seven years after its entrance into the funhouse of mirrors that is American law, it is impossible to deny the generosity of benefits it has showered on the American people. Young Americans are now able to remain on the family plan of their parents' policy until they reach the age of 26, smoothing their turbulent slide into independent adulthood. The ACA is responsible for the largest expansion of Medicaid in the history of the program, granting coverage to poor people at rates unprecedented in American history, and helping to reduce medical debt among Americans to an all time low. Thanks to those initiatives, along with the government subsidies helping middle and low income Americans purchase plans, twenty million people now have health care coverage who lacked it before Obama became the first president in fifty years to significantly reform his country's health care system.

Conservative critics of the program enjoy pointing out that insurance premiums have continued to increase in recent years, but they typically neglect to mention that they have increased at their slowest and lowest rates on record. At the same time, medical errors and hospital readmission rates have fallen to historical lows, because the ACA altered Medicare payment distribution. Rather than compensating hospitals for every procedure, without oversight or scrutiny, Medicare now withholds payments for operations or treatments made necessary by doctor errors or hospital failures.[17] Given that millions of people, for the first time, have access to medicine, pay reduced fees for that access, and can expect better treatments from an increasingly mindful and cautious medical staff, it is vomitous to witness the glee with which Republican commentators predict the 'collapse of Obamacare.' If Obamacare were to perish, millions of people would go to the grave right along with it, losing their health care coverage and heading back to the unmitigated market for medicine, which far more than any 'socialized' system in the rest of the Western world, rations according to wealth, employment status, and other financial methods of stratification. In transparent hope for Obama's failure, many right wing politicians and pundits display a set of perverse values that ranks political bragging rights over human welfare.

Nowhere is the nihilistic schadenfreude of the far right more visible than during the debate surrounding health care, and throughout the celebrations over certain health insurance carriers leaving the Affordable Care exchange market, where citizens can purchase private plans with public subsidy. Several companies, within five years, had left the exchanges in multiple states, making the claim that their participation was no longer profitable. As Obama has argued, this does present a problem, but not one that is unmanageable. Any major overhaul of the health care system with millions of participants is not going to function perfectly and seamlessly at any point, much less within its initial years of implementation. The withdrawal of carriers from state exchanges does not jeopardize the entire law, but it does demand correction. Just as flaws in Social Security, Medicare, and Medicaid were previously manageable by bipartisan problem solving and troubleshooting, so too are the ACA's weaknesses. The problem, then, is actually Republican negligence of the duty to govern, and more broadly, the corruption of health care distribution by the profit motive. While there should always remain a place for private insurers in the system, the demands of business should not hold hostage the needs of patients.

All evidentiary indicators, despite early problems, still indicate that the ACA is a success. The problems that do exist within American health care are a result of its insistence on market control. In another illustration of Gore Vidal's diagnosis of the nation with amnesia, large numbers of Americans protest against the costs of health insurance, as if prior to the passage of the Affordable Care Act, health care was not expensive. During the debate over health care reform in 2008, *Consumer Reports* documented that 76 percent of unemployed, uninsured Americans could not afford to purchase a plan on the private market. That number has dropped dramatically since the implementation of Obama's overhaul, due to the governmental subsidies for private buyers, and the enlargement of Medicaid availability. The same magazine described horror stories, such as the struggle of a Virginia retiree, who after making monthly premium payments for decades, could not find an insurer willing to cover him, because his doctor diagnosed him with diabetes. The Virginian's nightmare was hardly anomalous, but quite widespread before President Obama made it illegal for insurance companies to deny coverage based on pre-existing conditions.[18]

The Republican agenda to dismantle the Affordable Care Act will not only bring down havoc on the market, it will also cause undue pain and suffering in the lives of millions of Americans. The beneficiaries of Obamacare are not vulnerable to abstraction nor are they points on a poll measuring political popularity. When a man who lives two doors down from me received a grim diagnosis of lung cancer, he had no health insurance. In addition to dealing with the physical pain and emotional anguish of catastrophic news, he worried how he would afford treatment. That same afternoon a social worker in the hospital registered him for the statewide public health program made possible with the dollars President Obama allotted Indiana for Medicaid expansion. My neighbor, along with twenty million other people, has a higher quality of life, and simply has a life, because of government activism. Even as a moderate, who was often overly pragmatic, Obama expressed and exercised his mother's faith in 'position-paper liberalism.' In keeping consistent with his active-positive personality, and in deference to the lesson he learned on the bus ride back to public housing buildings fit for asbestos inspection, President Obama, more than his immediate Republican and Democratic predecessors, made an aggressive argument for the government's role in creating and maintaining a peaceful and prosperous society of hospitality and equality.

The stimulus package, regulatory agencies dedicated to protecting the integrity of transactions between people of ordinary means and institutions of extraordinary wealth, and the application of the law as an insurance of justice in the health care market, culminate to counter the extreme anti-government mood of much of the country. The right wing argues with the volume and elegance of a fire alarm that government is the cause of every evil, and the elimination of government will create utopia on earth. Ronald Reagan famously quipped, while missing the irony of occupying the highest office of government, 'Government is not the solution to the problem; government is the problem.' The so-called 'Reagan revolution' continues to afflict Americans, and not just those who operate out of right wing institutions and organizations. While it is certainly easy to find examples of mediocre bureaucrats who collect public salaries for producing little, if anything, of value, commentators should aim for the higher truth of recognizing how, in America's worst and best days, government has often acted as a civilizing force for human happiness and progress. The GI Bill, allotted for veterans of World War II, helped create the middle class. Public education acts as the foundation for middle class stability and lower class mobility in areas of America both rural and urban. During the horror of the 9/11 attacks, America took great comfort and found hope in the heroism of firefighters and first responders – public employees all. Instead of elevating images of public aid and enhancement of individual and communal life to a place of prominence in political debate, too many analysts resort to the easy cliché of government as corrupt and incompetent. Obama swung a counterpunch into the belly of the Reagan revolution, and its impact is most measurable with millennials, who consistently claim greater support for governmental intervention in social problems than their parents and grandparents. While America waits for the younger generation to enter roles of political leadership, it still must live with the consequences of having people who are hostile to politics define politics, and people who despise government influence government.

The virulent strain of anti-government fanaticism running through the body politic has moved the entire political discourse to the right. What was once conservative now appears liberal, and what was once liberal now appears unthinkable. Richard Nixon, as a Republican, increased funding for social welfare programs, signed the Environmental Protection Agency into law, and opened relations with China. Decades later, President Obama struggled to extend unemployment benefits, took half measures against high pollutant industries, and negotiated a deal against nuclear arms production in Iran while deflecting accusations of anti-American sedition and sabotage. Escalating distrust in public institutions, and suspicion of the role public institutions must play in the protection of civil society, manipulates much of the public into believing that public schools are not worthy of support, the government should not manage crises with policy, and that all politicians are equally corrupt. The absolutist position turns to paralysis, and builds a barricade on every path to progress. America arrived at such a dead end after years of anti-politics dogma with amplifiers coming from all sides, not just the predictable places. The paralytic and corrosive cynicism of anti-political and anti-government ideology helped clear the field for a Trump victory. Not only did he indict the entire 'system,' but he insisted that only someone with no experience, or apparently knowledge, within the system could solve America's problems.

Aristotle defined politics as 'matters relating to the city.' The city is the collective, and those who deny the collective – as Margaret Thatcher, the former British Prime Minister who is also a hero to the American right, did when she said there is 'no such thing as society' – can only commit arson in their roles as leaders of the collective. Bruce Bartlett, one of the few firefighters left in the Republican Party, recently relied on his experience working in the Reagan and Bush Sr. administrations to argue, in the words of his essay for the *American Conservative*, that 'Barack Obama is a Republican.' After reviewing most of Obama's policies, Bartlett concluded that Obama has 'governed as what used to be called a liberal Republican before all such people disappeared from the party.'[19]

Bartlett is correct in his identification of Obama as a centrist president, but overstates the case when he affixes a party label. Obama's ideology is as complex, and often contradictory, as his personality, but much of it exists under the concealment of cultural and political limitation. Presidents, for all their power and authority, are not dictators and cannot govern by fiat. They must navigate and negotiate the circumstances, crises, and conditions under which they rule. All leaders define their times, but all leaders are also defined by their times. Obama had to govern in an anti-intellectual and anti-government culture while facing unprecedented opposition from an organized party and persuasive lobby as vigorous as they are venomous. In that context, and in the tenor of those times, President Obama's policies and proposals were more comparatively conservative than those of Franklin D. Roosevelt, John F. Kennedy, and Lyndon B. Johnson. They were also much more liberal than the policies of Reagan, Bush, Clinton, and Bush. With an acrobatic skill for overcoming the restraints and restrictions he suffered, Barack Obama became the most effective and impressive advocate and agent of progressive politics in America. The 'position-paper liberalism' of his mother had no better enforcer than Obama. With his against-the-odds ability to conquer territory for liberal reform, while enduring an assault of political debris and cultural downpour, he became a transformational president. He marched into an area once thought off-limits, and established an opening for other liberals to follow. From every standpoint – political, cultural, moral – it is a major victory. It is only in reaction to his continual defeat of their best efforts that Republicans have some psychological justification for resenting the president. This is especially true considering that as Republican politicians and pundits became increasingly wild-eyed and erratic in their campaign to stop him, Obama remained calm, aloof, and good humored.

The tragic embarrassment of Donald Trump is impossible to understand outside of the Obama context. Trump's shocking acceptance, and tacit applause, of 'white nationalism,' a euphemism for bigotry, was due primarily to the eruption of white anxiety in the souls of his supporters, following the election and reelection of Barack Obama. It is not accident or coincidence that Trump decided to introduce himself to the political culture of America by becoming the most prominent spokesperson for the birther conspiracy theory. The forgiveness of Trump for his unapologetic expression of mean-spirited, borderline sociopathic, treatment of political opponents is the manifestation of the right's fantasy of destroying Obama, and everything he represents – multiculturalism, intellectual engagement, and progressive politics. If Obama were really the failure that many members of the right like to claim, voters would not have felt the need to anoint a boorish bully to bluster through the primary and presidential season. Trump is the opposite of the thoughtful, deliberative, and dignified Obama. For the right, he is a reaction to Obama, and a means of exercising their trauma in response to Obama. The success of Obama necessitates such an extreme reaction, and given Obama's widespread popularity among Americans under the age of 40, it will continue to influence American politics and policymaking.

It will take several years, if not decades, for Americans to truly appreciate the improvements Obama has helped author for America, in part because the cartoon depiction of Obama as a monster has too polluted the atmosphere for a generally disengaged and uninformed citizenry to see clearly. Compounding the tragedy of invisibility that defines the

Obama presidency is that most leftists refuse to celebrate the accomplishments of Barack Obama, the president, because they too cannot see Barack Obama, the person.

The official portrait of President Barack Obama

President Obama signs the Affordable Care Act

'Make America Great Again'

Martin Luther King: 'The arc of the moral universe is long, but it bends towards justice.'

Jesse Jackon in 1983

Barack Obama and Chicago Mayor Rahm Emanuel greet people on the tarmac at Chicago O'Hare International Airport, 2013

Jackie Robinson, the first African American to play in Major League Baseball in the modern era

President Obama announcing the My Brother's Keeper initiative

The Obamas

Harold Washington, the first African–American to be elected as mayor of Chicago in February 1983

President Barack Obama delivers a statement in the James S. Brady Press Briefing Room of the White House regarding the mass shooting at Sandy Hook Elementary School in Newtown, Connecticut, Dec. 14, 2012

Barack and Michelle Obama in 2008

Illinois State Senate Chamber, Obama's battleground

Mitt Romney, the Republican Party's nominee for President of the United States in the 2012 election.

John McCain, the Republican nominee for the 2008 US presidential election.

Bill Ayers

President Barack Obama with the Nobel Peace Prize medal and diploma

A Black Lives Matter protestor holding a photograph of Trayvon Martin at a rally

President Barack Obama attends the Sandy Hook interfaith vigil, December 16th, 2012

'Mister Hope'

Franklin Delano Roosevelt: 'We have nothing to fear but fear itself.'

rump: 'American carnage'

President Barack Obama giving the State of the Union address in 2014

Barack Obama and his vice president Joe Biden at Beau Biden's funeral

Obama sings 'Amazing Grace' while delivering Clementa Pinckney's eulogy

The inauguration of Donald Trump as president of the United States

Hillary Clinton campaigning in 2016

An election night event in 2016

THE MESSIAH

Sylvia Path, in one of her many masterful poems, 'Letters To a Purist,' likens the object of her scorn to a 'great idiot with one foot caught in the muck-trap of skin and bone,' and the other 'way out in the preposterous provinces of the mad cap cloud-cuckoo, agape at the impeccable moon.' What makes the poem brilliant is not Plath's condemnation of purity, and the purist's rejection of reality, but the residue of affection she still holds for that 'grandiose colossus.' Before addressing him as an idiot, she calls him 'my love.' The purist will always maintain appeal, because he speaks to everyone's conscience, and lives in a world – as fantastical as it is – that most people would like to inhabit, and would inhabit, if not for the corruption of that elusive and mysterious place so often condescendingly called 'the real world.'

At some point during the Obama presidency, perhaps in an attempt to keep pace with the far right, the hard left lost its sense of political reality. There has always existed a push-pull process between the more radical elements of the American left and the more conciliatory liberal aspects, but Barack Obama as a candidate, without the delivery of an overt homily, performed a wedding between them. While there were early skeptics of Obama, like Noam Chomsky and historian Paul Street, other socialists saw surprising potential in a mainstream politician. Cornel West campaigned aggressively for the Democratic Senator, Angela Davis, despite overwhelming evidence to the contrary, proclaimed that Obama 'identified with the black radical tradition,' and filmmaker Michael Moore did not give the typical, 'I support him but...' qualification to his emphatic endorsement, but offered a hearty statement of praise. Bill Ayers' eyesight was perfect 20/20 when he spotted the left's hallucination of the Obama wink: He might say he is a pragmatic politician, the hard left purist whispered, almost in the form of a prayer, and he might have the senatorial record of a slightly left of center, perfectly mainstream Democrat, but Obama is disguising his real identity and true intention. Without the same vicious assault and sinister delight, the far left performed the same erasure of Obama's humanity as the hard right. They made use of a prettier palette, but they too vandalized the Obama portrait.

In 2008, Barack Obama changed history before he even took the oath of office. He was the first black president-elect. Throughout the brutal and beautiful story of American politics and the enlargement of freedom, black citizens have consistently acted as a civilizing force in public life and law. The runaway slaves and the abolition movement made it clear that no country could claim to respect humanity while treating certain humans as property. The Civil Rights movement made it crystal clear – with moral pathos, political theater, and brilliant legal strategy – that no nation can call itself democratic, while a certain class or race is unable to vote, enjoy public accommodations, or exist as equals under the law. Without the humanizing influence of black citizens, American law, ethics, politics, economics, and pop culture are decidedly less free, fair, and fun. It is impossible to imagine an America that still enforces segregation, routinely disenfranchises all blacks, and lacks African American contributions to political rhetoric, education, religion, the arts, and popular movements for policy reform. The radical fact of a black man in the White House gave many liberal and leftist Americans the expectation that the policies from the new president would also constitute radical change. By picking up its own can of graffiti, and directing it at the Obama portrait, the hard left, like the far right, rendered Barack Obama invisible. He was not a human being, with a human history, but a clean slate and symbol onto which the left could project its own fantasies. Obama gave his inaugural address already surrounded by enemies and future enemies – the right wing committed to the distortion of his image into the phantasm of the monster, and the left wing crafting Obama into an angelic icon, unprepared for the inevitable disagreement and disappointment that would ensue when he revealed the slightest imperfection.

'Hope and Change' was the Obama slogan, and in his 'Yes We Can' address, he placed himself squarely in the tradition of the abolitionists, Martin Luther King, and the great movements of American history. His rhetoric was always aspirational and inspirational, but also vague. The atmosphere Obama created surrounding his campaign was slightly hazy, but beyond the beautiful cloud of oration, there was the clarity of Obama's advisors, policy proposals, and legislative history. At the earliest stages, Obama associated with key figures from previous administrations – primarily the Clinton team, but also one official from the Nixon years. Obama's specific statements of political ideology also demonstrated an entirely mainstream and predictable philosophy of soft reforms and liberal engagement of existing law. In the ascription of fantasies on the Obama frame, however, many Americans of the left believed he was a secret agent for their grandest designs and highest ambitions. Their fantasies – like many fantasies of sexual pleasure or commercial success – could not find satisfaction in reality. They became the standard of purity by which to judge Obama and, in the process, set him up for failure. There is no better example of the unreasonable pressure placed on Obama than his selection for a Nobel Peace Prize before he even executed an agenda. Obama was perfect on day one – like a student who has not yet turned in an assignment or taken an exam – and too many people believed his record would remain unblemished forever. Perfection is unattainable, and when Obama made errors or bad decisions, the hammer came down hard. The left would not only exaggerate his flaws and misread his motives to heighten suspicion, but also enforce a gag order on the mere mention of his achievements. The combination of censorship when dealing with the good and magnification when dealing with the bad became the preferred methodology of the far left, because to them, Obama was not only a president, given to success and failure. He was a liar, a saboteur sent from the 'establishment,' or in the words of Cornel West – 'a counterfeit progressive; a Rockefeller Republican in blackface.'

The rhetoric of West became particularly disappointing and delirious. For an otherwise brilliant intellectual to so profoundly hallucinate when looking at Obama gives a demonstration of how evaluating any president according to the irrational criteria of uncontaminated political and moral expectation will produce irrational behavior. There is an element of truth to West's more mild criticism, and the criticism that other leftists offer when accounting for the Obama presidency. President Obama did commit sins of commission and omission. It is important, even while guarding against the hateful lunacy of the hard right critique, to acknowledge and attack the failures of political priority, imagination, and will that took place throughout the eight years of the Obama presidency.

While Obama deserves great applause and acclaim for keeping the United States out of any major wars, even though he faced pressure from his military and political advisors to invade Syria, he made a foolish misstep when he approved of military intervention in Libya, and he has yet to thoroughly answer grave questions about the efficacy and ethics of his drone assassination policy. Studies from NYU Law School, Stanford Law, a UN investigation, and data collected by Glenn Greenwald for the *Intercept*, reveal that the majority of people who die in drone attacks are innocent bystanders. The US military and government has a long, imperial tradition of reducing the significance of innocent civilian death, in number and in moral terms, with the ghastly euphemism 'collateral damage.' Obama, in that sense, did not bring 'hope and change' in the slightest, but extended the cold and callous calculation of what Gore Vidal called 'the last Empire.' The drone strikes are a moral outrage, but they also renew inquiries into the consequences of 'blowback,' what the CIA calls the unintended consequences of foreign military intervention. The two mass shootings perpetuated by Islamic terrorists in the United States during 2016 were, according to the words of the murderers themselves, retaliation for the bombing of Afghanistan, Iraq, Syria, and other predominantly Muslim countries.[2]

Mark Mazzetti, a Pulitzer Prize-winning journalist who investigated Obama's 'secret army and war at the ends of the Earth,' concludes that Obama begrudgingly ruled over the drone regime; viewing the strikes, for all of their ethical and tactical problems, as a tolerable half step between pacifist isolation and the regime change, aggression, war hungry, torture friendly policies of his predecessor.[3] Obama campaigned as a peace candidate, won the Nobel Peace Prize, and held steadfast in his refusal to invade and occupy foreign nations. The drone strikes, including those against an American citizen turned terrorist, the intervention in Libya, and the escalation of Special Forces operations throughout Africa, give deadly illustration to the pressures on any president.

The Pentagon, the intelligence establishment, and the nexus of defense contractors can hardly handle a president unwilling to flex the muscle of American power around the globe, but American culture also acts as an influence. Polls consistently show that Americans are war hungry – supportive of bombing campaigns, torture, overseas assassinations, and even the invasion of Middle Eastern countries. In his own defense, Obama claimed that the drone strikes were conducted with the necessary precision for protecting American life from terrorist cells, while minimizing the risk of innocent death and injury. It is demonstrably true that in his second term, Obama radically reduced the amount of drone strikes. He also released documents demonstrating an almost laughably low civilian death count from the assassination policy. While the release of such numbers is a welcome reversal of the information blackout that typically characterizes the federal government's communication with the public on military matters, the dubious nature of the numbers raises questions about transparency and expediency. To his credit, even with the pressures of the Pentagon and public, Obama withdrew fighting forces from Iraq and reduced the remainder in

Afghanistan. The results are laudable, but in an exhibition of hypocrisy, ignored by the military-worshipping right wing. In 2010, the second year of the Obama presidency, 440 American servicemen and women were killed in action. In 2016, only one member of the US military died in battle.

It is almost impossible to imagine Obama successfully submitting to the public that the American military should have no international presence, but his own refusal to disengage, eliminate bombing, and deescalate Special Forces missions, shows enthusiasm in addition to capitulation. Twenty-nine cents of every American tax dollar goes to the military, and the US currently has over 800 military bases around the world.[4] Under the command of Obama, the American military bombed at least six countries, and conducted raids and other low-personnel missions in dozens of countries. Vidal predicted that the United States would cease to operate as an empire only after it ran out of revenue to fund it. It will take a cold and calculating conservative – not a principled liberal – who informs the public, 'It would be fun to keep blowing up the world, but we just don't have the money for it.' As depressing as it remains, the informed conclusion is that no president, no matter how well intentioned, will oversee an American disengagement abroad. President Carter came the closest, and he is considered a villain in many circles, and a failure in others, for his effort. Carter surpasses Obama in moral courage and intellectual honesty, and the difference – due to the larger failures of the American public – partially accounts for why he was a one-term president and Obama won reelection. The historical reality and political context does not excuse Obama, but it demands acknowledgement. After even the minimal reduction of American military presence, Republicans have routinely attacked Obama on the fallacious charges of 'depleting' or 'weakening' the military. Such an absurd attack indicates not only the insanity of the increasingly hawkish Republican Party, but also the intensity of the stranglehold that the 'military-industrial complex' maintains on the body politic.

The national security state uses the military as its enforcer, but also interferes in domestic politics. Obama was not prepared or willing to revoke or reduce its power. He enhanced whistle blower prosecution to levels not seen since Nixon, most famously in the threats of penalty against Edward Snowden, the former National Security Agency employee who went public with his knowledge of an extensive data-mining program. The United States government has access to every citizen's cell phone and email records, keeps them in a sophisticated storage system, and can comb through them should the need or desire present itself. For years, the Bush and Obama administrations respectively denied the existence of any program. Snowden not only exposed the lies of two presidents, but he also demonstrated that the extent of the program far surpassed anyone's imagination. It is a nearly universal truth that no president or prime minister voluntarily forfeits power. Many conservative supporters of George W. Bush defended his infringements on civil liberties, only to chastise Obama for the continuation of those same programs. Democrats who offered excuses for Obama might find themselves moonwalking to principle now that Trump has become his successor.

Another repetition of Bush foolishness to occur in the first term of the Obama administration was crisis mismanagement. In 2010, a BP oil spill off Louisiana in the

Gulf Coast became one of the most devastating ecological disasters in the history of the country. Ten conservation groups co-wrote a letter lambasting Obama for inexplicably waiting a month to aggressively respond to the catastrophe – precious time for the ecosystems and animal life under threat, and the fishermen who were out of work. Finally, Obama formed the Presidential Commission on the Gulf Oil Spill, which concluded that BP 'had not made a conscious decision to favor dollars over safety.' An investigative report in the *Atlantic* later found that the commission deleted a slide from its report showing that on eleven separate occasions BP did accept serious spill risks to save time and money.[5] The story vanished before any reporters had the opportunity to interrogate Obama on his knowledge of the slide, and if he was complicit in giving cover to a foreign oil company even after it endangered the American people and polluted American shores. While the BP oil spill does not rise to the unprecedented level of criminal negligence that Bush displayed after Hurricane Katrina, it certainly raises class questions over who receives legal protection from the federal government.

The same questions emerged bold and stark when Obama authorized bailout money, without restriction or supervision, for major financial institutions, but did not extend any assistance to community banks, credit unions, and other small lenders. There was a compelling economic argument for rescuing the big banks. Morally sickening or not, to allow the country's largest financial institutions to die would risk submerging the nation into a depression it had not seen since the 1930s. There was also a persuasive argument for throwing a lifejacket to small financial institutions, all of which would have gotten money on the street more rapidly and deliberately than the big banks. Small suburbs and country towns – often left out of economic calculation – would have benefited immensely from federal subsidy. The limping and heaving commercial districts of small cities like Gary, Indiana and Youngstown, Ohio might have turned such monetary medicine into salvation. Instead they never fully felt the healing hand of governmental intervention, and are left to fight their own way back to health.

Residents of California seeking marijuana for reasons of health or recreation found themselves in the unexpected and precarious position of ducking a supposedly liberal administration in Washington. While George W. Bush, much to the shock and chagrin of his conservative constituency, turned his back in the issuance of a 'hands off' approach to medical marijuana in California, Obama oversaw a federal prosecution of marijuana dispensaries, challenging state law and personal liberty. The inexplicable severity of Obama's anti-marijuana policy highlights hypocrisy, considering Obama writes at length in his memoir about the cloud of pot smoke in which he spent much of his late adolescence.[6]

Another oddity in conflict with Obama's biography is his pursuit of high stakes testing, merit-based pay education policies, often borrowed from the privatization fantasies of right wing saboteurs of public schools. In another continuation of Bush policy, Obama doubled down on the ideology behind the disastrous No Child Left Behind program, which reduced all learning to the passage of multiple choice examinations, and connected school funding to student performance on standardized tests.[7] The failure of the program is notorious, and it has become difficult to find anyone in education, at any level, who can offer even a modest defense of it. Obama has a history in education that should inform him of the dangers in relegating the classroom experience to exam preparation. He was a college professor in a field that necessitates critical thinking and creative argumentation, and as the right wing media delighted in reminding everyone, he served on a board with Bill Ayers that provided grants to schools innovating teaching methods so as to improve not only the outcomes, but the educational experience of children. Ayers believes that Obama's early surrender on education policy was an attempt at brinkmanship. Perhaps the president thought, 'If I give them education, they'll leave me alone on other issues.' It is highly speculative, but if that is the case, Obama failed twice – first politically, and second pedagogically. His administration accrued no rewards from adopting conservative ideas on education, and schools were the worse for it around the country. Due to a heavy strain of anti-intellectualism in American culture, political discourse is neglectful of education as a serious issue. Politically, economically, and culturally, it is easy to argue that education is the most important issue facing the future of the country.

Former Secretary of State, and current professor of history at Stanford, Condoleezza Rice said that there are such severe disparities in the public education system that it actually constitutes a long-term threat to national security. She also offered the fairly obvious observation that 'failing schools undermine economic growth... [and] social cohesion.'[8]

When confronted with a crisis, Obama not only failed to act with imagination and aggression, but he actually contributed to the perniciousness of the problem. The long term trends are moving in the right direction on some critical issues – the high school drop out rate is at its lowest point since the 1970s, and the college enrollment rate is at nearly an historic high. There is more to education than attendance and completion, however. In the words of George W. Bush, 'Rarely is the question asked: is our children learning?' The answer to that inquiry becomes tougher to articulate when surveys reveal profound ignorance among Americans on matters of history, science, and law, but schools continue to evaluate themselves based upon numerical scores on narrow examinations.

President Obama broke with his own destructive educational policy in his treatment of higher education. In his first State of the Union address, Obama – the first intellectual in office since Kennedy – explained that he would like to improve America's ranking in college attainment, laying out a series of proposals to assist more young people in their matriculation into colleges and universities. At that moment, the United States ranked twelfth in the world on the issue. It is now tenth. Obama also put an end to bank-based lending for students. His elimination of private lending, and transition to public lending, successfully lowered interest rates for borrowers, and allowed debtors to work out 'income-based repayment' rates so that their monthly bill would remain easily manageable. He also introduced debt forgiveness programs for graduates who enter public employment and work in the social services. He ended federal aid to 'for-profit' colleges that saddle students with unmanageable debt relative to their earnings, and finally, he created space in the public conversation for free college by proposing tuition-free community college. Both Bernie Sanders and Hillary Clinton took Obama's idea and ran with it in their respective campaigns, even broadening it to include public universities. For students already paying heavy bills to attend higher education classes, he increased funding for Pell grants (a federal aid program for students from low income backgrounds) more than any president in several decades.[9]

The left, with good reason, jumps at every opportunity to condemn Obama's record on primary and secondary education, but largely refuses to acknowledge that he, more than any president of the modern era, has done more to meet young Americans' desire, and increasing need, to acquire a university education. Education, as anyone with minimal historical and financial awareness understands, is the touchstone for societal equality and political progress.

Even a cursory look at the Obama record demonstrates that there are grand achievements to celebrate, but that there are also major mistakes and misdeeds to castigate. Obama's transgressions and errors were far fewer and softer than those of the human wrecking ball who preceded him, and his domestic accomplishments are, arguably, greater than any president of the modern era, but the left could not tolerate any imperfection from Obama. When he let them down, they let down all bearings of reason, and soon slipped into delirium. Just as the Obama administration brought about hysteria and paranoia on the far right, it also unintentionally initiated insanity on the hard left.

It is a strange and sad spectacle to see thousands of young Americans, who day-to-day study for degrees to advance into careers of their choice and express overall optimism about the state of the country and economy, cheer an elderly man as he announces that the 'system is rigged' against them. Just as strange as Bernie Sanders and his supporters, is the increasing popularity of the idea that 'there is little difference between the two parties' and condemnation of Obama for 'having done nothing.' Every single day Americans amplify the maudlin and overly dramatic declaration that 'politics is broken.' Despair and rage are the two emotions uniting both left and right. The respective camps indict different sources of the problem, and submit different solutions, but they are in general agreement with Bernie Sanders and Donald Trump that the country is 'falling apart,' the 'system is rigged,' and someone needs to incite a 'political revolution' to 'make America great again.' It is no accident or coincidence that the extreme and reality-resistant rhetoric of both camps so easily blends together. The slogans of the far left and the far right are interchangeable, and they both represent a hysterical worldview of decline. The right wing is generally easy to understand. They are losing their grip on the culture of the country, and are in a state of panic and anxiety over their loss of authority. The left wing is more interesting, because while Obama has done much to anger many of the left, conditions of the country under his leadership have largely improved. Those improvements should inspire more engagement and investment in traditional politics, not less, and they should strengthen the confidence of anyone with a liberal point of view. Why would the far left have such ridicule for a man who presided over the substantial decrease in poverty, the lifesaving increase in access to health care, the creation of regulatory agencies to better protect consumers and supervise financial institutions, and the injection of desperately needed revenue into local governments for the preservation of public employment?

The hysteria and paranoia of the left is not entirely mysterious to me, because I once espoused it. In 2012, months before Obama's reelection, I wrote an open letter to Obama supporters for the radical journal, *Counterpunch*. As an attack from the president's left, my letter urged readers to support the Green Party candidate for the White House, Jill Stein. I ran through the laundry list of complaints and grievances reasonable liberals and leftists should have against Obama (see above), but instead of recognizing his achievements, and acknowledging his virtues, I offered the litany as the totality of his presidency and personhood. I also seemed to have forgotten everything I learned about the complexity of civics and American government, including the coursework I did at a fine university to acquire a degree in political science. My criticisms of Obama were fair, but the conclusion that his flaws and failures are all that exist is not only uninformed and irrational, but one that assumes he has dictatorial powers. Any president operates with the restraints of a three-branch system of governance. Obama not only had to contend with that institutional constriction, but also fight unprecedented opposition from the Republican Party, and deal with an American culture collapsing into anti-intellectual hostility to nuance, subtlety, and historical awareness. The American people, like those inhabitants of Elkhart, Indiana, continued to grow more pessimistic, even as their cities and states grew more stable and prosperous. How was Obama to persuade Americans, who polls consistently show rarely read and know little about history? And how was he to appeal to Republicans who believe he is the antichrist, secretly sympathetic to terrorists, a closet communist, or all of the above?

Reckoning with these questions is essential work in the task of unpacking the presidency of Barack Obama. I ignored them, because it is intellectually easy and morally satisfying to exercise the sanctimony of the purist, but also because Obama's status as first black president rendered my critical faculties comatose. Like Angela Davis, I believed that because Barack Obama was the first black president, and because his ascendancy was made possible by the black freedom movement, that, regardless of what he said or did, he was part of the black freedom movement tradition, and he would usher the principles and practices of the black freedom movement into the White House. If Obama were white, his failures would exist in context on the left. If he were just an average white Democrat – nothing spectacular in the story of American improvement and development, the analysis of his presidency would follow a predictable rationale:

He is a mainstream, moderate to liberal Democrat who is responsible for some positive reforms, like the Affordable Care Act and regulations on Wall Street, but because he is part of the two party system of power in Washington D.C., he also possesses the same problems of policy and imagination that other politicians in high ranking roles display on a daily basis. On the ground organization is essential to control presidents with conservative ideas, but also cajole presidents with progressive instincts. Voting is an important act of citizenship, but because it is not the ultimate act of citizenship, it requires calculation. The 2016 Republican Party platform included an endorsement of therapy to convert gays to heterosexuality, measures aimed at the censorship of pornography, and massive tax cuts for the wealthiest Americans. The Democratic Party platform included tuition-free college at public universities for any student from a household with an annual income under $85,000, and lowering the entry age of Medicare from 65 to 55. There are major differences between the two parties, and to behave otherwise is to welcome the further destruction of the social safety net, civil society, and participatory democracy in the United States. There are also canyons of dislocation in the duopoly that include eerie similarities on military spending, foreign policy, and loyalty to corporate America. It is possible to politically walk and chew gum at the same time.

When I wrote my open letter to the left in 2012, I lost my ability to intellectually multitask. Fortunately, my audience was small, and I had no influence on the outcome of the election. I also had no influence on myself. Standing in the voting booth, and looking at the available names, I voted for Obama. Something powerful happens to the citizen when actually confronted with the choice – the gravity settles in your stomach. It is partially for this reason that the election of Donald Trump remains so shocking. Millions of Americans drove or walked to the polls, stood in line, and actually cast a vote for Trump. One of the reasons he won, however, is because many other Americans, citing disapproval of various decisions and moves Hillary Clinton had made, stayed home, or voted with the Green Party. In crucial swing states, the gap between Obama's turnout and Clinton's turnout was enough to elect Donald Trump. Refusal to vote for Clinton illustrated the mentality of the purist, and the irrationality of the Obama critic. Progressive resistance to Clinton was dependent on the same arsonist indictment of the 'rigged and broken system' that began during the Obama years. Forget that Obama secured health care access for millions of people, and kept the country out of war. Someone has to 'shake up the system.' The anarchist streak that grew during the Obama years found a home in Bernie Sanders' rhetoric, and eventually led key voters away from the ballot box. Donald Trump certainly noticed. During one of his Hugo Chavez style victory speeches, he credited Democratic voters who stayed home as 'almost as good' as the people who pulled the lever for him. Those absent citizens will have to live with the consequences of their tantrum.

Barack Obama, by no fault of his own, destroyed the rationality of the left. An assumption of radicalism crowded its collective mind – Because his election was transformative, and a major victory for freedom and equality, his policies would follow with equal power.

There is a striking scene in *Invisible Man*. The narrator has begun to speak in white neighborhoods about civil rights and black residential and commercial rights in New York. A white woman of beauty and grace approaches him at the end of his lecture, clearly captivated with his presence and presentation. She invites him to her home, and he accepts. Sitting on the couch, she asks him more questions about his cause. Under the assumption that she, despite their racial differences, shares his passion, he speaks with great care and conviction. They soon retire to the bedroom to have sex with each other. The protagonist is then awoken by the appearance of the woman's white husband in the doorway. He requests that his wife wake him up early in the morning, and after she agrees, he lets out a sardonic laugh. The narrator waits for the husband to leave the room, quickly gets dressed, and makes a mad dash for the door. As he walks home, he vows that he will make sure to never sleep with a married woman again, but also gains the painful realization that his seductress had no real interest in his ideas, biography, or humanity. He was only a sexual fetish for her, a tool to satisfy her body and curiosity. The husband's informed laughter revealed as much, and the feeling of pride and pleasure he felt in sexual triumph soon morphed into shame and sadness over his continued invisibility.

Just as many conservatives demonized the president, many white liberals fetishized him. In an avoidance of his humanity, white liberals believed that Obama could become the instrument of their political pleasure; a tool for the edification of their own ideological fantasies. In a country where for much of its history the very state of black existence was radical and subversive, surely the first black president is radical and transformative. The white woman in *Invisible Man* saw the narrator as a sex toy, and nothing more. Not all, but many white liberals in America saw the president as a symbol, and nothing more – a symbol for American progress and change. Symbols don't disappoint, and don't err from that which they symbolize. When President Barack Obama became a human being, the answer for many of the left was not to analyze him as a human leader within the context of the culture and structure he must navigate and govern, but to erase him from consideration, and conclude that the entire country, in spite of decades of political progress toward liberty and justice, was teetering over the edge of Armageddon.

If the first black president cannot make everything perfect, the illusory ideology seems to state, then nothing will ever improve. The absence of Obama from consideration in the national conversation about American development is bizarre, but indicative of an ideological convenience. Because the president is responsible for significant improvements in the quality of millions of people's lives, he complicates the increasingly popular notion on the left that the United States is the capital of deprivation and exploitation.

When I cast my first vote for Howard Dean in the Democratic Primary race of 2003, sixteen percent of American adults were uninsured. Now, a mere seven years after passage of the Affordable Care Act, it is down to nine percent. When I cast my first vote, the United States was simultaneously prosecuting two major wars. Now, the United States conducts morally reprehensible and tactically questionable bombing operations, but the American military is not occupying any foreign nation. When I cast my first vote, the president of the United States went on the record to deny the existence of climate change. Now, there are bold regulations in procedural practice to radically reduce greenhouse gas emissions. When I cast my first vote, gay marriage was unthinkable. Now, it is legal. When I cast my vote, I had no idea that soon the entire economy would crash due to lack of regulatory supervision over Wall Street. Now, oversight is in place to prevent the reoccurrence of financial collapse. These are significant moves. They certainly do not solve every problem or end every injustice, but they are worthy of acknowledgement and applause. Instead of celebration, what occurs is desperation – desperation in the attempt to act as if the United States has leaped the calendar to move from 2008 to the present. The Obama presidency, despite all reports to the contrary, did exist, but its success rendered it invisible to the right wing, while its moderation erased it from view of the left wing.

The vandalism of the Obama portrait and distortion of the Obama persona is most clear on the intractable conflict of race and racism. While the right wing ignored everything Obama actually did and said, and imagined that he was Louis Farrakhan, the left wing seemed to believe that, as a beneficiary of the civil rights movement, he would generate a new power source for black freedom; taking advantage of his historic and unique role of 'first black president' to lead America into a 'post-racial' paradise.

Michael Eric Dyson, one of the most powerful and prolific American intellectuals, argues in his book, *The Black Presidency*, that one of Obama's worst and most wicked failures was a betrayal of his black base of support. He spoke in harsh tones of condemnation in black churches, according to the ordained minister and college professor, and he refused to advocate and legislate public programs of assistance 'targeted toward the black community.' Unlike West, Dyson provides a much more thoughtful, nuanced, and balanced assessment of the first black president. Dyson's sharp analytical apparatus, and grand poetic style of rhetoric, gives him much to appreciate in Obama's demonstrably positive influence on American politics and culture. He does, however, echo some of the criticisms of Obama when he calls for 'targeted' assistance toward black neighborhoods. Poverty relief programs, such as the Affordable Care Act, relieve the hardships of poverty for all people. Some black leftists miss that truth, just as some rural white voters missed it when they voted for Trump, despite his promise to repeal Obamacare, and in doing so, restrict their own access to health care. White conservatives believe that Obama has done too much for black people, and in the process shown contempt for white Americans, while black leftists, like Dyson and West, feel that Obama has done too little. It is impossible, in every sense, for both of these things to be true.

The reality is that Obama, likely due to his own complex ethnic ecology, is a peacemaker on racial conflict. He grants that animosity and hostility from whites toward blacks is a structural and cultural impediment to racial justice and equality, but as he told one predominantly black audience, 'you can't use racism as an excuse to justify your own failures.'

In his famous address on race during the 2008 campaign, he respectfully denounced and distanced himself from both the ideology of his grandmother and his preacher. The elderly white woman in his childhood, almost by generational default, advocated racial stagnation and separation. The elderly black man in his adulthood, almost out of self-protection, advanced an idea of black nationalism antithetical to American unity and individuality. The left rebuked Obama for his criticism of his preacher, and the right accused Obama of slandering his grandmother (as if they knew her) for political gain. They both failed to recognize that Obama's is a position that pushes and pulls at both sides of the color line, and tragically, one that satisfies few people. White Americans, easily the most sensitive people on the planet, cannot tolerate even the mildest recrimination, while the most hardline of black activists interpret any censure against their purity as an act of ancestral treason.

As first black president, Obama failed to conform to any of the pre-scripted and choreographed roles America allows for powerful black people. There is what Shelby Steele calls the 'challenger' role – the loud, morally strident firebrand in the tradition of the black church and civil rights movement. The challenger is what the hard left wanted, and was disappointed not to receive. It is also what the far right feared, and hallucinated into optical existence. Also available to black Americans is the role of 'bargainer.' Steele explains that the bargainer is he who promises to never confront white America on their historical sins and present errors, as long as he is allowed to do what he chooses. Louis Armstrong was a bargainer; Miles Davis, a challenger. Jesse Jackson is a challenger; Clarence Thomas, a bargainer. Obama oscillated between challenge and negotiation, often even presenting an unlikely test for black America. Because most Americans accept the binary categories of identity available to black leaders, whites assumed that because he is not a bargainer, Obama is a challenger, while left wing blacks believed that because he is not a challenger, he is a sell-out bargainer. The bridge between the two positions, as Obama has likely learned after valiant effort, is not ready for construction. Obama attempted to act as engineer, but became invisible in the eyes of most of the public.

Michael Eric Dyson makes a compelling argument that Obama's refusal to directly challenge white America sensitized whites even further against any critique. The Obama insistence on coddling whites dramatized even subtle discourse of racial exploration. Obama's mundane and benign observation that Trayvon Martin, a black teenager killed by a racist vigilante, 'could have been my son,' provoked outrage among many whites, who hallucinated Obama's diplomatic figure into Louis Farrakhan storming the podium. David Remnick, biographer of Obama, recalls the president telling him that when he addressed race, even the wrong word selection, could 'enflame' the entire country. The 'color line,' as W.E.B. Dubois called it, remains dangerous to navigate.

There are two great divides in American history, and they persist in the present conditions on the ground: black versus white, and rich versus poor. Obama did much to bring all groups closer – economically and culturally – but the American people were not ready for post-racial movement or post-partisan progress. The right refused to even acknowledge the humanity of Obama, while much of the left adopted an irrational hostility to his policies. Bernie Sanders, during his candidacy, could not utter one sentence without using the phrase 'income inequality.' The gap between rich and poor has become an area of intense focus and interest for the left. Considering the obsession with division between the haves and have nots, which began with the Occupy Wall Street demonstration, it is bizarre and boneheaded that the hard left, Sanders included, never mentions that the Congressional Budget Office concluded in June of 2016 that Barack Obama has done more to fight inequality than any president of the past fifty years. Obama spent more money on anti-inequality programs than any president since Lyndon B. Johnson, and the results are entirely predictable. Rates of inequality have returned to the pre-recession, pre-Bush levels of 2000. In 2015, the median income increased at the highest rate in a single year on record with the poor and middle class showing greater gains than the wealthy. After eight years of Obama in the White House, more Americans are financially stable and comfortable, more Americans have access to medicine, and fewer Americans are dying in unnecessary wars overseas. The alternative universe of political reportage and commentary verifies the indictment Barry Glassner issued against America's 'culture of fear,' when he wrote, 'Americans will take any happy ending and turn it into a disaster story.'

The hard left and right both committed to dystopian depictions of America, and for the survival of their politics and the health of their acumens, had to act as if Obama's accomplishments did not exist. Barack Obama became the invisible president, because his visibility would act as a direct refutation of the doom and gloom hysteria of most American activists and analysts. The oft-repeated phrase, 'Trust in American institutions is at an all time low,' has become a bromide of American discourse. Polls indicate that it is, generally, true. It then becomes important to ask – Doesn't it seem more than coincidental that faith in American government eroded quickly after a black man became its most visible leader?

The only rational answer to that question reveals the reason for part of the nationwide skepticism of Obama, even that which clouds the judgment of the left. It also demonstrates why one group in particular has maintained a clear focus and rational disposition in reaction to the Obama presidency.

The same polls demonstrating a nearly national consensus that America is slipping into a nightmare also reveal that black citizens are among the most hopeful. They consistently demonstrate optimism on issues of the economy, race relations, and long term potential for personal and political improvement.[10] Hope among African Americans remains high despite the outbreak of police shootings against unarmed black men that have darkened headlines and polluted neighborhoods in city after city throughout the Obama presidency. As many historians and journalists have observed, the injustice of police violence against racial minorities is nothing new, but the technology that captures the crime has brought new attention to the problem. From attention comes action. As counterintuitive as it seems, all of the news is almost cause for hope in the face of fear. It is certainly better to have an open debate on disaster than to allow the disaster to worsen without scrutiny (one can only speculate as to the degree of white insanity that would ensue if black police officers began gunning down unarmed white men).

It is painful and brutal to acknowledge, but footage of agents of authority assaulting black Americans is an ordinary, unsurprising supplement to the story of the black experience in American life. Given the long struggle for freedom, and the intimacy with institutional oppression, in African American history, black citizens have an informed perspective on politics, power, and progress. Norman Mailer once observed that while there are many unintelligent black Americans, just as there are with any group, there are no stupid ones. Black history gives every lucid black American a sophisticated awareness of how American mechanisms of influence operate at levels of governance and culture. White Americans, contrarily, have lapsed into a state of delirium, all but forgetting the fundamental facts of history, politics, and economics. Having no sense of history, they believe that America, despite record highs in standard of living and near record lows in crime and poverty, is a post-apocalyptic hellscape. They react to their hallucination with a demand for immediate transformation. Because problems still exist, the prevalent mindset seems to submit, nothing is getting better. African Americans see progress and injustice side by side, and assimilate that contradictory proximity into their long view of the world. Obama is an important and powerful piece of the moral landscape.

President Obama brought with him the African American awareness of politics, power, and progress to the White House. Like any president, his record is full of fault and failure, but unlike many presidents, his resume also boasts of significant accomplishment. Black Americans comprised his most loyal base of support, partly because he was their champion. He achieved what no other black American had ever achieved, and thereby attracted an investment of pride and faith. The investment did not merely attract symbolic returns, but paid in policy. Obama's reversal of criminal justice developments is a powerful example. No president has done more to combat mass incarceration, or generate energy for the movement to rehabilitate, rather than incarcerate nonviolent drug offenders. Black Americans, as indicated by their optimism, also understand the negotiation that exists between the slow pace of progress, and the higher hope of history.

Jesse Jackson, who ends every speech with the words 'keep hope alive,' but is far from a naïve daydreamer, once told me that 'sometimes when you are climbing out of a hole, you get so focused on how far you have left to go that you forget to look back to see how far you have come.' Jackson himself has seen the movement he helped lead morph America from an apartheid state where blacks could not even vote to a genuine republic where blacks can become mayor, governor, and president. Despite dramatic progress, Jackson still dedicates himself to justice and equality on a daily basis. Voting is essential, but it is only a tool in the achievement of an American architecture that welcomes and shelters all with equal liberty and opportunity. The Obama presidency proved a useful application of that tool, but far from sufficient in the overall assignment.

Martin Luther King, Jr. disavowed gradualism, but he certainly understood that every victory, no matter how crucial, is gradual. Ending segregation would not kill racism. Gaining public accommodations would not destroy bigotry. Stopping the Vietnam War would not end all violence, conquest, and death of the innocent. As much as it frustrates and flummoxes, progress demands diligence and patience. President Obama, no matter how much the futile protests of leftists suggest, could not, and more importantly, would not end every injustice. He could and has helped reduce suffering in America, and improve the communal standard of living.

From the day that he announced his candidacy for the presidency to his final moments in office, Obama often returned to what he claims is his favorite quote from Martin Luther King. The words decorated his desk in the White House, reminding him of his inspiration, and the reality of history, always at once reason for celebration and despair. Millions of Americans would do well to issue themselves the same reminder: 'The arc of the moral universe is long, but it bends towards justice.'

A PRESIDENT WITHOUT A COUNTRY

In a town hall discussion of criminal justice reform, racism, and police brutality toward black neighborhoods, President Obama with a jovial grin and jocular tone referred to himself as 'Mister Hope.' He then offered a characteristically optimistic survey of the future in an attempt to bolster the hope of his audience in the room and in millions of living rooms across the country. The next day the town hall, which was broadcast on public television and network television, showed no measurable impact on the mood or beliefs of Americans.[1]

Since his emergence in national politics, Barack Obama has earned the reputation as the most calm communicator and rational deliberator in the modern history of the presidency. Seemingly impossible to rattle, he always managed to lower the temperature of the room, deploying the reason of history and the logic of professorial analysis, to relieve the hypertension of a public in perpetual panic. He was the doctor with a smooth and soothing bedside manner, but he was continually sent into an examination room with a hypochondriac off his meds. How does a doctor ease the worries of a patient who does not want to get better? How does Mr. Hope ingratiate himself to a crowd of cynics and audience of alarmists?

These questions take on profound and particular importance considering that Obama understood the Kennedy wisdom of the superiority of words over deeds when it comes to public persuasion. Biographers and associates agree that Obama first discovered his voice as a community organizer offering hope and direction to impoverished residents of Chicago neighborhoods, but that voice grew stronger and gained distinction with each elevation of Obama's political career – from a local leader to a state official, from a state official to a national senator, and from the Senate to the presidency. Political scientists have documented how American culture might have entered a twilight zone of postmodern, post-persuasion stagnation. Because Americans are increasingly bitter in their polarization, and because the largely positive development of Internet destruction of monoculture, has led to the negative tendency of people to seek out only information that confirms their pre-held biases, millions upon millions of citizens are no longer susceptible to variation of ideology. They don't change their minds, because they are not curious about anything that might change their minds. On the rare occasion that they confront commentary contrary to their beliefs, they grimace, shake their heads, and walk away, already placing it through the partisan filter. Under these conditions, the president becomes a bizarre figure. Behind the bully pulpit, it is almost as if he is just another pundit. Obama's task became one of even greater difficulty considering that he used the rhetorical tactics of the professor and the black minister – figures who communicate from the respective orientations of intellectual rigor and hopeful pathos. The Americans he most needed to convince are anti-intellectual, suspicious of education, and committed to an all-encompassing pessimism. Nowhere was the Obama oratorical struggle more clear than on the quiet salesmanship of his foreign policy.

After a series of terrorist attacks in Europe, and mass shootings in the United States, President Obama addressed the crimes and catastrophes as demanding vigilance, but took time to remind Americans that the world is actually at its least violent in history, and that crime rates in the Unites States are at their lowest since the 1970s. Immediately, Obama faced harsh criticism from television commentators on Fox and CNN, columnists from major newspapers, and countless citizens on Twitter. It was hard to find even casual acknowledgement that all of the available data supported the president's statement. One of the divides that proved difficult for Obama to breach was the preferred method of inquiry separating him and the general public.[2] While Obama often cites data to underscore his assessment, the general public operates according to an internal hierarchy where facts rank below feelings. Obama's accurate analysis of historic reduction in violence, both at home and around the world, was irrelevant next to the emotional, public perception that the world is more dangerous than ever before.

When President Obama made a historic gesture and change of policy toward Cuba, opening relations and making an official delegation to the small, island nation off the coast of Florida for the first time since 1928, a terrorist bombing occurred in Brussels. Republican officials, political pundits, and ordinary Americans amplified admonitions of Obama for not cutting his trip short. They argued that he should return to the United States to address an attack in a foreign country. Sitting with his Ray Ban wayfarer sunglasses in the stands of a Cuban baseball game, Obama addressed the criticisms directly during a live on air interview:

> It is always a challenge whenever there is a terrorist

> attack anywhere in the world. I want to be respectful of the lives lost and to the gravity of the situation, but the whole premise of terrorism is to disrupt people's ordinary lives. We have to show strength, courage, and resilience in the face of these attacks. They cannot defeat America or the Western World. They don't produce anything. They don't have a message that appeals to the majority of people in the world, or the majority of Muslims. What they can do is scare us, disrupt our daily lives, divide us. As long as we don't allow that to happen, we will be fine.[3]

'We will be fine' is a mantra many Americans should repeat at the turn of every hour. All of the other messages they deliver and receive seem to suggest otherwise. In a sad and grim turn, America has gone from a nation that accepted the wisdom and leadership of 'We have nothing to fear but fear itself,' during the Great Depression and World War II, to a collection of cowards angry that the president has the temerity to observe that the world is getting better, and that small groups of terrorists are unlikely to end civilization.

Delusional despair and apocalyptic panic, most of which comes from aging whites, dominates far too much of the dialogue in American culture and politics. Donald Trump, in perhaps his only clever calculation, seized on the depression with his indictment of America as a 'hellhole' and promise to 'make America great again.' At the surreal, science fiction inauguration of President Trump, he continued his bleak assessment, breaking with inaugural tradition to celebrate American democracy with assurances of unity and hope. Flailing his arms around with the Capitol behind him, Trump described 'American carnage.' While Americans express terror over every potential threat, no matter how slight, from every corner of the globe, no matter how isolated, they display the symptoms of national Alzheimer's, seemingly forgetting that during the Cold War the entire world was within inches of nuclear holocaust. Two World Wars almost destroyed civilization, and what amounts to just a second on the historical clock, fifty years ago, the United States was in Vietnam where approximately 58,000 soldiers died. The world, by any objective measure, is much safer and more stable today. Freedom House reports that more nations have democratic forms of government than ever before, and rates of interpersonal and social violence are at low points. American foreign policy should reflect positive developments, rather than imagine enemies and panic at the sight of one's own shadow.

The foreign policy of the Obama administration emanated from the steady temperament and clear focus of the man most instrumental in crafting it. George Bush, Dick Cheney, and Donald Rumsfeld depicted a world in chaos, and crafted a policy to control the chaos – regime change, the invasion and occupation of hostile countries, and consistent violation of international law. The interventionist aggression of the Bush administration only made the world more violent and less stable. While Obama committed the error of enhancing the drone strike policy, and although he admits that his largest mistake was to accept the advice of his State Department and invade Libya, he had largely taken a deep breath and stepped away from war, military adventure, and American interference in international conflict. He negotiated a nuclear arms deal with Iran that would successfully stop them from pursuing the manufacture of a nuclear weapon. The deal is not perfect, as a few of its key conditions have an expiration date, but it does create a window of opportunity to assimilate Iran into the world of peaceful nations, and demonstrate why cooperation is more beneficial than combat. The Iran deal is, predictably, treated as an invitation to another Holocaust by most Americans. Trump promised to 'rip up' the deal, calling it the 'worst he ever saw.' Obama eased the embargo against Cuba, helping to make peace with a nation that has done nothing to harm the United States since the early 1960s, and in his most significant and intelligent maneuver, he resisted unanimous calls for another stupid and destructive war in the Middle East.

In 2012, when Syrian leader Bashar al-Assad launched a vicious assault against his own citizens – violating human rights and international law – there were thunderous demands for the United States to invade in a humanitarian operation. Obama, perhaps in a bad bet, tried to quell calls for war, while appearing tough, with the issuance of a 'red line.' If Assad used chemical weapons, Obama warned, the United States would take military action. It was an imbecilic choice of words, and it has, with some just cause, become a monumental embarrassment for the president. Soon after Obama's bluster, Assad did use chemical gas against innocent civilians, including children. Every one of Obama's military advisors argued that he had no choice but to declare war on Syria, leading officials in the State Department echoed the military position, and most major newspapers editorialized that, as loathsome as it seemed, another war was necessary. President Obama begrudgingly nodded, and his Secretary of Defense, along with the Joint Chiefs of Staff, began drawing up battle plans. Press reports started to circulate that America, for the third time in eleven years, would wage war. At the last second, according to one White House insider, 'the president blinked.' His blink allowed him to regain clarity of vision. Was saving face and keeping up appearances after a regrettable threat worth the lives of thousands of Americans, trillions of American dollars, further escalation of violence in an already hostile region of the world, and continued terroristic blowback against America for military infringement of Islamic culture?[4]

The answer was as clear as burning money and bloody bodies, and Obama's decision to prioritize lives, dollars, and long term stability over abstract notions of American honor and authority, was a touchstone moment of his presidency – a demonstration of the power of rationality over the emotional convulsions that too often dictate American policy and dominate political debate. The United States of America is not at war right now because of Barack Obama. That is a reality that demands greater respect and bolder articulation.

Given the volume and force of American drone strikes, the invasion of Libya, and the escalation of military raids throughout Africa, it is impossible to argue that Obama earned his Nobel Peace Prize, but he did reduce the imperial aim of America, and he drew down the tactics of war. In a parting gift to citizens around the world who prize peace over murder, Obama commuted the sentence of Chelsea Manning, the former soldier who released footage of Americans brazenly killing innocent civilians in Iraq to Julian Assange for publication on WikiLeaks. The military justice system sentenced Manning to thirty-five years in federal prison. Because of Obama's brave commutation, she served only three years and ten months of her sentence. Her heroic actions exposed a war crime, and for Obama to show leniency toward her, allowing her to experience freedom, gives dramatic demonstration to how Obama, while far from a pacifist, attempted to distance America from its enthusiasm for war.

President Obama, however, was in a cultural war of his own. His enemy was the American people, and as his culture continues to detach itself from his values and principles, he occupied an odd and unprecedented position. He was a president without a country. He did not acknowledge his adversarial status in America. In keeping with his ongoing theme of optimism, he argued that the American people 'vindicate his hope.' Typically, he made stirring statements offering tribute to his country in a room full of adoring fans. His rhetoric appears to have triumphant impact on the audience, and gives the impression of unanimous approval. In the summer of 2016, however, polls demonstrated that seventy percent of Americans believed that the country was 'moving in the wrong direction.' Obama attempted to articulate the moral cosmology of Dr. King. Too blurry to identify because of the far distance at which it might happen, the arc of the universe will bend toward justice. In fact, it is already in movement; visible at some angles, but at other angles of iniquity, the movement is so incremental that it becomes invisible to the naked eye. The American people, despite having one of the highest standards of living in world history, have come to reject faith in political progress, requesting their own excommunication from the church of humanism. Obama is archbishop.

It is not that Obama is without persuasive success. He can claim one of the greatest cultural achievements of the modern era. When he entered office, patriotism was solely the property of the right wing. Demagogues and reactionaries deployed the language of national pride to shame dissent and silence criticism of American foreign policy. The Bush administration thrived on their creation of a repressive atmosphere in which nearly any rebuke of Bush national security policy was met with accusations of 'anti-Americanism.' Beginning in 2004, with his famous keynote address, Obama initiated a continual redefinition process, turning patriotism into a liberal principle. He engineered the infusion of Whitman poetry into politics, at once resurrecting and regenerating the notion that America is worthy of love only because of its virtues of diversity, hospitality, and opportunity, not because of its supposed, but inevident, economic and cultural superiority. Obama invited further right wing hatred, by exposing their nationalism as an empty scam, and gave accurate forecast of a country in motion. Rapid diversification of demography, the liberalism of young Americans, and the loosening mores of mainstream culture proved the president correct. The right wing reacted with resentment not only to Obama, but to the country that twice elected him, and in an unprecedented implication of American decline and failure, nominated and elected for president a cynic with the slogan, 'Make America great *again*.' Despite the Trump victory, studies and surveys consistently reveal that young Americans support the America of Obama's presentation. Nationalism conquered American government when Trump won the presidency, but as the loser of the popular vote with an unprecedented disapproval rating, he is not an accurate representation of dominant American attitudes.

In his conquest of the American center, Obama defeated the right wing. He also continually made fools of them as they became increasingly extreme and paranoid in their opposition and articulation, and he maintained the good-humored calm of someone entirely indifferent to their best efforts. Despite its tragic themes, Ellison aimed to imbue *Invisible Man* with what he called 'blues-toned laughter.' 'Could it be,' Ellison asks in an introduction to his masterpiece, 'that there is a subtle triumph hidden in such laughter... one which still is more affirmative than raw anger?'

During the 2016 State of the Union Address, President Obama announced, 'I have no more campaigns to run.' The Republican representatives and senators in attendance rose to their feet, and in a typical exercise of immaturity, began to holler and applaud. Obama, forced to stop in mid-sentence, gave the cheers a few seconds, smirked, and then retorted, 'I know, because I won both of them.' He embarrassed Republicans, and rather than doing it with a painstaking, point by point defense of his record, or an angry admonition, used wit to taunt lesser opponents, giving illustration to the affirmation of blues-toned laughter. Obama's oratorical brilliance and strategic savvy vastly exceeded that of Republicans, and he was not only of a different race, but younger. Most Republicans are white, and most are over the age of 55. Barack Obama, through laughter and dry humor, dished out routine humiliation to older, white men – the very constituency once with uncontested cultural authority in America.

Norman Mailer, in his seminal essay on John Kennedy, 'Superman Goes to the Supermarket,' explained that presidents not only have political effect and economic impact, they have cultural influence. More than a policymaker, commander, and executive, the president, for better and worse, is an emotional director for the country's culture. In addition to the empowerment of specific constituencies, presidents also – through use of language, prioritization of ideas, and temperament – push American culture until it tilts in one direction.

Mailer writes that Kennedy had a 'good and sound liberal record,' but the real reason to treat his political emergence with excitement is that he 'has a patina of that other life, the second American life, the long electric night with the fires of neon leading down the highway to the murmur of jazz.' Because Kennedy, with his Hollywood looks, his sexual vitality, his charisma, and his high level wit, offered illustration and assertion of the underground, second American life, he had the potential to become an 'existential hero,' and America, according to Mailer, is a nation that needs heroes. The stiff and stale 1950s opened up the antiseptic space for Dwight Eisenhower to act as hero, but he was a hero for that large number of Americans who, in the words of Mailer, 'were most proud of their lack of imagination.'

Eisenhower, and his political party, represented the America of 'church ushers, undertakers, choirboys, prison wardens, bank presidents, small-town police chiefs, state troopers, psychiatrists, corporation executives, Boy Scout leaders, head nurses, and the fat sons of rich fathers.' Kennedy represented 'glamour over ugliness,' but also pleasure – the America of Walt Whitman, Bessie Smith, and Elvis Presley.

Barack Obama had two, grand cultural ambitions when he entered office. The first was to widen the American identity and reinvent the idea of American patriotism. He succeeded. The second was to rehabilitate Americans, after eight years of Bush madness, into hopeful and rational people. He failed miserably.

Obama walked into a culture of dread, paranoia, and hysteria in which people project their personal fears and frustrations onto politics. He could not shift American society toward hope, because the pervasive despair is not a political problem. It is a psychological one with political manifestations. Thirteen percent of Americans take anti-depressant drugs, and according to the World Happiness Report, the US now ranks fifteenth in overall satisfaction among the world's populations.[5] The suicide rate continues to climb, while the divorce rate remains high, and the American Sociological Association reports that with each year Americans claim to have fewer friends that they can call 'close confidantes.' [6] A recent poll indicated that 70 percent of Americans are 'disengaged from their work.' [7]

People who hate their jobs, because the work seems empty, are taking legal measures to escape their painful marriages, don't have many friends, and try to ease their personal misery by swallowing medication, are not likely to view their country, or the world, as safe, healthy, and happy. Instead, they will project their own neuroses, anxieties, and frustrations onto politics, believing that if they are dissatisfied, unfulfilled, and emotionally malnourished, the world must be crumbling down. American politics has become a therapeutic transference opportunity for people already sad and angry. Misery loves company, as the old expression goes, and if someone is personally unhappy, he might take comfort in the fantasy that the world is politically unhappy.

Then, Obama makes his smiling and waving entrance to announce, with an array of factual evidence at his disposal, that the nation and the world are actually getting better, and will continue to improve if calm, kind, and rational people collaborate to enhance the public interest and common good. This is not a message miserable people are going to welcome with open ears and arms, because its buried implication is that if you are unhappy, it probably isn't the world's fault. It just might be yours. President Trump tells his voters that their problems are everyone's fault but their own. Mexicans, Muslims, the Chinese, and a frightening cabal of elites all conspire to restrain his constituents from the achievement of their dreams. The Trump theme of despondency and devastation is music to the depressed citizen's ears, especially when he promises to 'fix it right here and right now,' as he did in his inaugural address.

When President Obama explained that the world was less violent and more free than ever before, and that the future was full of promise, he was attempting to lead a people shut off from leadership. Americans want to hear that the world is a global disaster zone, because anything more hopeful fails to resonate with their angst. Barack Obama was the political and moral director of a nation in existential crisis. Angst, according to the great existential philosophers and novelists, is the fear and dread that results from the experience of human freedom and responsibility. Freedom provides people with choices, and in turn, makes them responsible for the consequences of their choices. The depiction of America as dystopian alleviates the anxious of their fear that they are responsible for their own misfortune or discontent. 'The world is so bad right now I have no choice but to...' the depressed citizen reassures herself, and then fills in the blank with whatever routine or decision brings them grief. Jean-Paul Sartre called this self-imposed limitation, 'acting in bad faith.' Whenever a free individual convinces herself that she 'has no choice,' she surrenders to a bad faith claim. The reality is that, even when circumstances or pressures make the choice difficult, even painful, she has the choice, and therefore, has more power over her life than she acknowledges.

Obama's vision and message of hope tells people to exit from America's culture of fear, ignore 'if it bleeds, it leads' news coverage, and aggressively follow the revolutionary mandate for the 'pursuit of happiness.' It presents doubt in the face of bad faith. It offers the empowerment of the self and the affirmation of agency. If the world is good, and if the future is pregnant with possibility, freedom becomes a blessing, not a burden. People who have abused or misused their freedom will shrink from that story, and rise for the depiction of a world as a giant crime scene. Victims are not responsible for their victimhood. Few observers have made the connection, but 'yes we can' is as much an existential tenet as it is a political slogan. A country committed to 'no we can't' is not likely to react well to 'yes we can.' It was a winner during the 2008 campaign, but after Obama took his rightful place in the Oval Office, and the average American's loneliness, dissatisfaction, and alienation remained present in the mind and heart, it became less an optimistic creed than a psychological taunt – 'I'm miserable and this black guy keeps telling me everything is fine.'

An operative word in the Obama slogan was 'we.' The pronoun of plural responsibility and participation contrasts violently with Trump's narcissistic, paternalistic assurances –

'I alone can fix it,' 'I will never let you down.' 'We' appeals to people who feel secure in their purpose and potential. Trump's leadership model demands passivity, and comforts those who suffer from what Jimmy Carter called 'a crisis of confidence.'

The way in which Obama tells it also presents a problem for much of America. The former president, more than any of his modern predecessors with the possible exception of John F. Kennedy, is effortlessly elegant. He injects a literary panache into political rhetoric, making him unique at his moment, and rare in the motion of history. Over the course of the past few decades, America has become less eloquent and more vulgar. A continual debasement of language has infected the body politic and broader culture, creating an opening for political candidates, like Donald Trump, who in addition to the use of crude invective, according to various studies, speaks at a fifth grade level. It has also led to the dominance of political discourse through mediums like cable television and Twitter. Shorthand, slogans, and shouting prevail over serious analysis and argument. Simple language, even to the point of inarticulate sputtering, is now comfort food for many Americans. It makes them feel assured and at home. Eloquence challenges Americans. It paints a picture of a complex world, and in doing so, confronts listeners and readers with the test of elevation. Jesse Jackson once explained that leadership requires the leader to never speak down to the audience, or even meet them where they stand, but to speak above them, elevating them to higher intellectual, moral, and political ground.

Ralph Ellison wrote that one of his goals as artist and novelist was to 'endow inarticulate characters, scenes and social processes with eloquence.' The essentiality of eloquence is indisputable, because the interests of art and democracy converge at the point of articulation. 'The development of conscious, articulate citizens is an established goal of democracy,' Ellison explains, 'and the creation of conscious, articulate characters is indispensable to the creation of resonant compositional centers through which an organic consistency can be achieved in the fashioning of fictional forms.' Literature is what Ellison calls a 'symbolic action, a game of as if,' but, like politics at its best, it is also a 'thrust toward the human ideal.' Eloquence expresses the ideal, while vulgarity violates it.

If America were a novel, Barack Obama would make for an effective and fascinating protagonist. Readers could learn of his story in *Dreams from My Father*, and continue on to read the complicated hero narrative of a man's rise from community organization to national leadership, ascending to previously unknown heights by breaking a glass ceiling. Literary enthusiasts would move chapter to chapter, learning of the struggles of a man who finds himself in an adversarial position against his culture, and seeks to rise to each occasion, pass each test, and win each war with only the armament of eloquence.

The novel, *Invisible President*, would not have to follow a chronological order. It could begin with a prologue. The unnamed narrator, currently acting as chief executive of the country, has just learned of the death of his close friend's son, who himself was also a friend. The close friend – the father of the deceased – is also his vice president. Beau died at the young age of 46 from cancer. He was a combat veteran, an attorney who focused on the prosecution of sex crimes against children, and a successful Attorney General in his home state of Delaware. He planned to run for Governor, but the indifference of the universe ran deadly interference.

The Invisible President is tasked with the unenviable and painful assignment of offering consolation to his friend as eulogist at the funeral, but because of his unique authority in America, his eulogy will double as communication to a nation torn apart with despair, civic strife, and social mourning. Headlines of police killings and killers, threats of terrorist attack, and routine massacres by firearm pollute the atmosphere, creating unrest and the impression of danger around every corner. The unnamed narrator must choose his words carefully. He has to honor his friend, but he is also set for another sparring match with a culture increasingly anti-intellectual, vulgar, and cynical. How can he not only comfort the bereaved, but also counter the killjoys and misanthropes? How can he act as communicator-in-chief and consoler-in-chief to inculcate doubt against bad faith, giving birth, in its place, to faith in future possibility?

The Invisible President steps up to the podium in an old, creaky Catholic cathedral, face worn down with grief and eyes heavy with the task that awaits him.

> 'A man,' wrote an Irish poet, 'is original when he speaks the truth that has always been known to all good men.' Beau Biden was an original. He was a good man. A man of character. A man who loved deeply, and was loved in return.
>
> Without love, life can be cold and it can be cruel. Sometimes cruelty is deliberate – the action of bullies or bigots, or the inaction of those indifferent to

> another's pain. But often, cruelty is simply born of life, a matter of fate or God's will, beyond our mortal powers to comprehend. To suffer such faceless, seemingly random cruelty can harden the softest hearts, or shrink the sturdiest. It can make one mean, or bitter, or full of self-pity. Or, to paraphrase an old proverb, it can make you beg for a lighter burden.
>
> But if you're strong enough, it can also make you ask God for broader shoulders; shoulders broad enough to bear not only your own burdens, but the burdens of others; shoulders broad enough to shelter those who need shelter the most.
>
> To know Beau Biden is to know which choice he made in his life.

It is a eulogy doubling as an existential cry for empowerment – action in the face of adversity, pride and passion in the face of pain, conviction in the face of cruelty. The only certainty that exists in life is death, and death is always a harvester of sorrow. In a nation incapable of dealing with the tragic, and inventive of the traumatic, overreacting to real sources of grief and imagining future sources of mourning, the Invisible President asserts precisely what Albert Camus called the 'revolt against absurdity.' When the world, and life, appear intrinsically absurd, creating catastrophe at random, and bringing death to the door of the good, the young, and the just, the only solution is not to act as if comprehension is possible, but to revolt and rebel. Beau Biden, after losing his mother and sister in a car crash, invented a life of insurrection against arbitrary madness. The Invisible President turns the tragic funeral into a celebration, and offers the deceased as a template for the free life. Originality and authenticity – honesty and integrity – become the self-sustaining substances of struggle against internal despair and external defeat.

Throughout all of the nation's collective anxiety attacks over every possible problem, large and small, the president offers a reminder that when literally the worst happens – the death of a child – there still exists the opportunity to make claim on the potential of life, liberty, and the pursuit of happiness. The American promise is an affirmative one, and it is not for the passive or panic-stricken. Fighting back tears, chin quivering when making reference to family – that topic that always most shakes the protagonist president – he closes the clasp on the chain, connecting American history with human identity.

> Anyone can make a name for themselves in this reality TV age, especially in today's politics. If you're loud enough or controversial enough, you can get some attention. But to make that name mean something, to have it associated with dignity and integrity – that is rare. There's no shortcut to get it. It's not something you can buy. But if you do right by your children, maybe you can pass it on. And what greater inheritance is there? What greater inheritance than to be part of a family that passes on the values of what it means to be a great parent; that passes on the values of what it means to be a true citizen; that passes on the values of what it means to give back, fully and freely, without expecting anything in return?

> That's what our country was built on – men like Beau. That's who built it – families like this. We don't have kings or queens or lords. We don't have to be born into money to have an impact. We don't have to step on one another to be successful. We have this remarkable privilege of being able to earn what we get out of life, with the knowledge that we are no higher than anybody else, or lower than anybody else. We know this not just because it is in our founding documents, but because families like the Bidens have made it so, because people like Beau have made it so.

Later in his remarks, the narrator would return to Patrick Kavanagh, that Irish poet whose wish for the bereaved was that grief would become a 'fallen leaf at the dawning of the day.' The Invisible President then advised the Biden family, through their heartache and trouble, to 'think about the day that dawns for children who are safer because of Beau, whose lives are fuller, because of him. Think about the day that dawns for parents who rest easier, and families who are freer, because of him.'

The will to regain some semblance of control over life as executed through the assertion of freedom is what the president is preaching. It is Mister Hope at his most philosophical and literary; fully embracing and expressing the complicated and burdensome reality that melancholy and joy are always interconnected. One cannot exist without the other. Death has made his love for a friend more urgent, and he communicates the urgency of love and liberty to his audience in the church and through the country. The eulogy resounded through the cathedral halls, but it remains unclear if it registered in the country. America still appears at panic and in paranoia, but some work takes decades to enter into visibility. Perhaps, the author of that work will soon become visible too.

The tradition with the most philosophical wisdom and democratic weight in American life is that of the black tradition. Barack Obama occupies a unique position in that tradition, because his presidency was impossible without it, but his individuality is removed from it. Raised by his white mother and relatives, and coming of age outside of black America, his lineage traces directly to modern Africa. He is not the descendent of slaves. He is, however, a man with an intellectual awareness and an emotional sensitivity to history, including his role and place in it. The black tradition in American life forms out of struggle, and narrates, harmonizes, and rhapsodizes revolt against absurdity; rebellion against the cruelty of bullies and bigots, and the often harder to handle kind that is all too random. The president never marched, suffered a beating, or took a bullet to win the right to vote. He only won enough votes to become the most important symbol and success of black franchise. It is an odd and unprecedented contradiction that prevented him from speaking for the tradition, but enabled him to speak with it.

Obama danced perfectly to the rhythm of the black tradition – a blues beat of pain meets a gospel refrain of hope – when he delivered the eulogy for Reverend and State Senator Clementa Pinckney. He did so in the context of the tradition that animated Pinckney's life long after it made it possible. He spoke about the functionality of the black church as an institutional headquarters for the Civil Rights Movement, and the Underground Railroad before it. He was there in a storied black church not merely to offer an elegy for a man who dedicated his life to public service, but to address a nation in horror and mourning. Pinckney and nine of his black congregants were murdered in a vicious crime committed by a racist killer named Dylann Roof. Roof, a young white man, attended an African American church Bible study session, and near the meeting's conclusion, opened fire on the very people who welcomed him with smiles and open arms.

Outside of the service where Obama spoke, Jesse Jackson told a radio interviewer that it was significant that they were standing on Calhoun Street – 'It is named after a slaveholder, and it runs right into Meeting Street, where they sold our people. This place is dripping with a kind of indecency, a kind of barbarism. I mean, slavery, 246 years, was real. And the extension of slavery was even worse, in many ways, because at least slavemasters tried to protect the health of their slaves enough for them to work and reproduce. But after slavery, when slavocracy lost to democracy but kept the political and military power, 4,000 blacks were lynched, 163 lynched in this state without one indictment, often carried out by judges and police.' [8]

Roof's violence was not only one of immediate death, but also an act of symbolism that resurrected the memory of historic death. As the air dripped with barbarism, and America attempted to navigate its way toward sanctuary, Roof brought back into view all of the torment and trauma of racist brutality, issuing a reminder that, even with the incalculable gains toward justice and equality, history is inescapable. Obama, as he occupied the podium, was symbolic of victory over history. If indecency poisoned the atmosphere outside the church, Obama's presence sanitized the air inside with the rewards of faith, and the promise of the future.

Obama again had to meet a challenge – speaking in two voices at the same time. He had to harmonize his consolation for the mourners in his presence, and his leadership for the anxious in his country. His entire presidency existed behind a veil of race, preventing most Americans from clearly seeing his humanity and political philosophy, and now he stepped into a blood stained setting of America's ongoing racial battle. He began with a recitation of his favorite message:

> The Bible calls us to hope. To persevere, and have faith in things not seen. We are here today to remember a man of God who lived by faith. A man who believed in things not seen. A man who believed there were better days ahead, off in the distance. A man of service who persevered, knowing full well he would not receive all those things he was promised, because he believed his efforts would deliver a better life for those who followed.

Pinckney's example, according to the president, is that the dedication of one's self to 'feeding the hungry' or 'housing the homeless' is not 'just a call for isolated charity, but the imperative of a just society.' It is this belief that a just society exists beyond the horizon that inspires and enlivens anyone willing to work toward it, and it is the only shield that exists against the bullies and bigots of the world, who seek to erase any imprint of hope for future generations. Such an erasure leads only to the paralysis of cynicism, and the subjugation of every spirit to a solitary cell of darkness and dread. When

Americans continually express and reinforce the belief that there is no cause for hope, and that disaster and devastation await around every corner, they surrender to the likes of Roof, and step closer to the long nights in that cell.

Pinckney, and those who died at his side, represent another vision for the world, and it is this vision of progress and triumph, even in the most tearful moments of troubled times, that the president aimed to emphasize in his eulogy. Without that vision, President Obama would not exist, and the chains that held the ancestors of Pinckney's church members bound would have never broken. After detailing the brutality of slavery and segregation – the barbarism that Jackson felt and smelled and sensed in the air – Obama delineated the beauty of 'we shall overcome,' 'keep your eyes on the prize,' and most of all, 'amazing grace.'

> It would be a refutation of the forgiveness expressed by those families if we merely slipped into old habits, whereby those who disagree with us are not merely wrong but bad; where we shout instead of listen; where we barricade ourselves behind preconceived notions or well-practiced cynicism.
>
> Reverend Pinckney once said, 'Across the South, we have a deep appreciation of history – we haven't always had a deep appreciation of each other's history.' What is true in the South is true for America. Clem understood that justice grows out of recognition of ourselves in each other. That my liberty depends on you being free, too. That history can't be a sword to justify injustice, or a shield against progress, but must be a manual for how to avoid repeating the mistakes of

> the past – how to break the cycle. A roadway toward a better world. He knew that the path of grace involves an open mind but, more importantly, an open heart. That's what I've felt this week – an open heart.
>
> That, more than any particular policy or analysis, is what's called upon right now, I think, what a friend of mine, the writer Marilyn Robinson, calls 'that reservoir of goodness, beyond, and of another kind, that we are able to do each other in the ordinary cause of things.'
>
> That reservoir of goodness. If we can find that grace, anything is possible. If we can tap that grace, everything can change.
>
> Amazing grace. Amazing grace.

Obama, without care for his flat voice, then broke into the old, gospel hymn, giving rise to the entire congregation who helped him hit the high notes. They got through the hard parts together.

In *Invisible Man*, the unnamed narrator feels a great possibility of self-discovery and empowerment when he recognizes his gift for oratory. 'I could reach the very top,' he explains, 'even if it meant climbing a mountain of words.' He continues in comparison of himself with the great abolitionist leader, Frederick Douglass.

> For now, I had begun to believe, despite all of the talk of science around me, that there was a magic in

> spoken words. Sometimes I sat watching the watery play of light upon Douglass' portrait, thinking how magical it was that he had talked his way from slavery to a government ministry, and so swiftly. Perhaps I thought, something of the kind could be happening to me. Douglass came north to escape and find work in the shipyards; a big fellow in a sailor's suit who, like me, had taken another name. What had his true name been? Whatever it was, it was as 'Douglass' that he became himself. And not as boatwright as he'd expected, but as an orator. Perhaps the sense of magic lay in the unexpected transformations.

Barack Obama talked his way from a poor neighborhood in the South Side of Chicago to the presidency. It was an unexpected transformation for the man, and for the country. It was as orator that he first discovered himself – speaking in church basements and living rooms to his community activists and advocates, and then at the Democratic National Convention in 2004. It is as orator that the real Obama seemed to emerge throughout his presidency, giving America a glimpse into the substance behind and beyond the hope; the intellect and imagination connected to the emotion.

When Barack Obama sat silently in the White House crafting policy, he ceased to exist. One side of America believed he was plotting the destruction of everything they hold dear, while many others believed he was helplessly prostituting himself for a corporate bidder. As orator, Obama emerges through the fog and offers to America a singular vision of American patriotism, substantive hope, and the yes-we-can-do spirit that fortified the black freedom movement, and carried him across the caverns of fatherly abandonment, poverty, and confusion to familial strength, achievement, and leadership. As the Elvis of American oratory in the 21st century, Barack Obama elevated political rhetoric to performance art. It could have given Americans something to which they could aspire, but instead too many got lost in a miasma of bitterness, fear, and resentment. The lost souls and minds elected Donald Trump, and even then, Obama remained steadfast in his dedication to hope. 'The only thing that is the end of the world is the end of the world,' he remarked in his final press conference before adding, 'I'm mad, and I'm frustrated, but at my core, I believe we are going to be ok. We just have to work and fight for it.'[9]

Barack Obama as policymaker and political administrator is complicated. He is worthy of celebration when he enabled millions of Americans to enjoy access to health care, or when he rescued a damaged economy from depression. He is worthy of condemnation when he advanced the imperial presence of the American military, or when he further weakened the public education system. His legacy will demand praise and fond remembrance, but like any president, he will not escape history without a little dirt on his clothes and blood on his hands.

When a reporter requested his own thoughts on his legacy, he maintained his resolute faith in future progress. His answer offers the immortality of art. A great speech – like a great song or a great novel – lives long after its creator dies. If America was not yet prepared for the strength and substance of Obama's hard won hope, maybe younger citizens will someday return to the president's words, make the speaker visible, and more important, make their country a healthier and happier place to live.

I've tried to use my voice and my influence to raise issues to the surface, frame issues, and help people work on important issues. I do so with the hope, and belief, that because of the work we're doing now, not just Malia and Sasha, but their children, will enjoy a freer and more just world. We can't solve every problem and right every wrong, but that's okay. No one can. We plant seeds, and it is someone else of another generation, who will sit under the shade of the tree we planted.

AFTERWORD

From Obama to Trump: An Examination of American Psychosis

A wall cloud is a large, ominous cloud that hangs low to the ground, acting as the launching base of a tornado. The overwhelming majority of wall clouds do not form funnels, and most funnel clouds do not touch the ground. Even in the heartland of the United States – a region with the nickname 'Tornado Alley' – tornadic activity is relatively rare. Far more severe storms fail to produce twisters than those that succeed.

Throughout the final months of 2015, and throughout most of the year in 2016, a poisonous, black wall cloud loomed large over the American landscape. Forecasters and meteorologists continually reassured a frightened public that it would not produce a cyclone. Then, when from the wall a large funnel formed, those same experts, who have spent decades studying similar weather patterns, insisted that there was little chance that the funnel would reach the surface below. On November 8, 2016, a tornado touched down and tore through small towns and major cities in the United States. The only questions that now remain involve the severity of the storm. Will it rise to the level of F5 – spawning 300 mile per hour winds, reducing any structure that stands in its way to rubble? Is it possible to contain its devastation, or will the destruction, and debris it throws around, cause power outages, ceiling collapses, and explosions all over the world?

The election of Donald Trump to the presidency

remains surreal. On election night, as the numbers began to indicate that the unthinkable would occur, feelings of depression, rage, and confusion swept through at least half of American homes, and buried themselves in the chests of billions of people on every continent. The painful irony of America's first black president putting his legacy in the hands of a candidate who received the endorsement of the Ku Klux Klan, ran an overtly racist and nativist campaign, bragged about committing sexual assault, and demonstrated alarming ignorance on matters of history and public policy, is difficult to describe.

Barack Obama and Donald Trump are perfect opposites. While Obama is diplomatic to a fault, Trump, under the auspices of 'political incorrectness,' routinely insults foreign powers, journalists, critics, and citizens of different ethnic and religious backgrounds. Obama is a learned, cultured man with a cosmopolitan appreciation of the world, and a nuanced application of patriotism. Trump is a crude nationalist who displays delight in rhetorically challenging the global communion of nations. Obama's administration was remarkably free of scandal, and without even the hint of corruption. Before Trump even took his oath of office, his conflicts of interest and foreign entanglements appeared so debilitating that several of America's most prestigious professors of constitutional law argued he was unfit to serve. In his early years, Barack Obama worked as a community organizer in one of the nation's poorest and most dangerous neighborhoods, fighting for asbestos removal from public housing, improvements to local schools, and targeted investment from nearby businesses. Donald Trump earned his formative experiences helping his father fight off allegations of racial discrimination against African Americans in his apartment buildings. Barack Obama wrote one of the most sophisticated and sincere memoirs in the past thirty years of the genre, and spent his presidency giving masterful exhibitions in rhetoric. Beyoncé once credited Obama with the compliment, 'He makes me want to be smarter.' It is impossible to imagine anyone making a similar claim about Trump, who misspells common words on Twitter, and who linguists claim speaks at a middle school reading level.

Just as the depth of the disappointment in watching America transition from one of its most elegant, intelligent, and optimistic leaders to its least qualified, most vulgar, and most cynical is difficult to describe, it is also hard to understand, especially for the culturally illiterate punditry. It did not take even days for political commentators and analysts to condemn Barack Obama as an 'ineffective politician,' partially assigning him blame for the monstrosity of Trump. Because Obama failed to adequately defend his achievements, and effectively promote his agenda, many editorialists insisted, the country drifted rightward to a demagogue who cradled the emotions of those who felt 'left behind.'

In America, democracy is considered sacrosanct, and therefore, criticism of the 'demos' – the electorate and general public – is at once taboo and blasphemous. Heretics who violate the religious doctrine protecting the sanctity of the American people suffer social shaming and political fallout. Mitt Romney's candidacy for the presidency imploded when footage leaked of him criticizing the '47 percent' of Americans who do not pay taxes as not having an open mind to his economic argument for lowering the tax rate, and also seeking government handouts to support their lifestyle.

Romney's first point is perfectly logical. It stands to reason that people who do not pay taxes will not include tax policy in their criteria for selecting a president, while the second is not only more debatable, but condescending and closed-minded. Hillary Clinton suffered a similar fate when she derided half of Trump voters as a 'basket of deplorables.' I remember once when I was on a Chicago radio show, discussing the potential of a Trump nomination, I stated the obvious by accusing Trump of organizing a xenophobic campaign. The host raised a pathetic protest, 'But millions of Americans support that campaign.' Yes – the two are not mutually exclusive. It is not only nonsensical, but morally irresponsible, to condemn a candidate for bigotry, misogyny, or any other offense against decency, but excuse the voters who make that candidate's victory possible. If throughout the Republican primary, Donald Trump registered at single digits in the polls, no one would discuss him at any length. It is only because he galvanized such fervent and faithful support that he became president, and that he simultaneously fascinates and horrifies the entire world.

Barack Obama has lived as an invisible man for eight years, and now in a cruel turn of history, America has elected a man president on the promise that he will erase many, if not all, of the marks Obama made on American policy, law, and political procedure. The nullification of Obama's legacy is the continuation of his invisibility. It is impossible to delete him from American history, but if America can render his influence and accomplishment invisible, it will make it seem as if the first black presidency never happened. If one is willing to get shut of sentimentality, it is clear that such an ugly reversal of social and political progress is not Barack Obama's fault. It is the American people's fault.

Obama faced accusations that he was to blame for the flatulent rise of Trump, and easily deflected them in a press conference with his usual combination of amusement and bemusement – 'I have been blamed for a lot of things from Republicans, but to be blamed for who they select in their primaries is novel...It is fair to say that Republican media has been feeding the Republican base the notion for seven years that everything I do should be opposed, compromise is betrayal, maximalist positions on political issues are advantageous, and there is a 'them' versus 'us,' and 'them' are responsible for all the problems 'us' are facing. I don't think I was the one to prompt questions about my birth certificate. I don't remember saying, 'hey, why don't you ask me about that? Why don't you question whether I'm American?' So, what you are seeing within the Republican Party is the success of all of the efforts creating an environment in which someone like Donald Trump can thrive.'[1]

Obama then suggested that Republicans take time for some 'soul searching.' For all of his brilliance, he might as well have suggested that they all immigrate to Antarctica. He also recommended that the 'serious' conservatives who still exist, and who opposed Trump at the time, 'reflect upon what it is about the politics that they've engaged in to allow the circus we are seeing to transpire.'

It is too narrow to affix blame for the development of Donald Trump solely on the Republican Party. Everything that the former president said is correct. Republican officials, and their base, along with right wing media personalities, and their audiences, have become rabid in their defiance against reason, multiculturalism, and moderation, but the circus did not cease to transpire in the general election. Hillary Clinton made many campaign errors, but she did aggressively and impressively prosecute the case against Trump's experiential, intellectual, and temperamental fitness for high office. Over 62 million Americans – not all of them tin foil hat wearing right wing conspiracy theorists – dutifully stood in line, approached the ballot box, and cast their vote for Donald Trump to lead the nation. The cultural, institutional, and individual failures that made such a nightmare possible include, but also transcend the 'cracking up,' as Obama called it, of the Republican Party.

There was an awkward moment for Hillary Clinton during the campaign when she momentarily lost her otherwise impenetrably steely surface, and exposed the frustration that she, likely more than anyone, but also tens of millions were feeling. In a video address to her supporters, she ran through the litany of mean-spirited and stupid remarks Trump had made in the previous months. These included his call for a ban on Muslims seeking to enter the country as immigrants, his denigration of a Muslim American family whose son died during combat in Iraq, his mockery of the appearance of several women journalists and political spouses, and his assertion that a judge's Mexican heritage disqualified him for presiding over a case with impartiality. As she reached the end of the recitation, her eyes bugged out, and she shouted, 'Now having said all of this, why aren't I fifty points ahead?'

As predictable as ever, the mainstream media mocked and maligned Clinton's unscripted moment of anger. Her question, however, was the most important of the entire campaign, and it becomes of even greater concern in retrospect. Why didn't the American people roundly reject the unqualified, bigoted, chauvinistic, and uninformed candidate to deliver a landslide victory to the qualified, egalitarian, and brilliant candidate? To contextualize the campaign from that angle is to open up the important inquiries. Instead of wasting time on the obvious tactical missteps of the Democratic National Committee, such as Clinton's unwise neglect of Michigan and Wisconsin, there is an imperative that the nation comes to grips with what the triumph of Trump exposes about itself. Rather than parsing over the poor outreach strategy of the sane candidate, Americans should consider why so many of their fellow citizens felt comfortable empowering the insane candidate. In yet another irony, the same America that rendered Barack Obama invisible, became visible with the election of Donald Trump.

There are many elements to American psychosis, but central to the diagnosis is the symptom of racial resentment and anxiety. An unintentional gift that Trump has given the country is that his success has removed the mask of white civility. It is a mask that hides the face of a monster. When many white Americans politely discuss diversity, or discipline children for the use of racial epithets, they are maintaining a façade dependent upon the protection of their authority. As soon as people of color start setting terms for coexistence, suddenly the mask comes off, and a beast comes out. Currently, the beast wears tanning spray and sports a hideous comb-over, but he is a beast all the same, and he and his aggrieved coalition of Caucasians threaten to devour years of social and political progress.

The Republican Party, much of the mainline press, and even influential forces within the Democratic Party, like Senator Bernie Sanders, attempted to conceal the reality of racism in the 2016 presidential election almost immediately after Clinton's concession. The preferred narrative took shape as identifying opposition to 'free trade agreements' and 'globalization' as the primary motivators of Trump voters. The story self-destructs under even the slightest scrutiny, but that is not about to stop Americans from amplifying it. It makes people more comfortable, especially in their unrealistic sentimentality about American life, than the truth.

It is undeniable that free trade, even though, or more to the point, because Americans know almost nothing about it, is unpopular. Ball State University conducted a study finding that since the passage of NAFTA in the early 1990s, only thirteen percent of jobs lost were due to trade. Over eighty percent of jobs disappeared because of automation – a development that will only continue to spread, leaving many Americans – unwilling to acknowledge reality – unprepared and confused.[2] Arguments over trade, given how much it generally benefits workers and consumers, are important, but largely moot with Trump voters. Polls demonstrate that the majority of voters whose main concern was the economy voted for Hillary Clinton. A large majority also believed that the former Secretary of State and Senator was better equipped to engineer economic improvement.[3] Trump voters, no matter how much the mainstream media presents them as the modern-day Joads, were not primarily concerned with the economy. The same polls proving that Clinton won economic-minded voters also reveal that over half of Trump voters believed that 'diversity comes at the expense of whites,' the federal government gives too much help to black people, most Muslims sympathize with terrorism, illegal immigrants are a plague killing the country, and Barack Obama is a closet

Muslim who might not have been born in the United States. Truly a basket of deplorables.

The American pundits and journalists with loudest microphones and largest audiences tend to live in New York or Washington D.C., and have degrees from Ivy League institutions. They should celebrate and speak with pride about their achievements, but they might also want to realize that because Harvard Yard and Manhattan do not typify the American experience, they miss crucial cultural factors when attempting to comprehend and explain current events. I live in a small town in Northern Indiana. While my hometown is not any more 'American' than New York, it does give me an advantageous vantage point for determining why so many white people were eager to enlist into the Trump personality cult.

I grew up in Lansing, Illinois – a small town thirty miles south of Chicago. For most of my 1990s childhood, the ethnic and cultural variety of Chicago did not permeate my hometown. Lansing was almost entirely white. Neighborhood events were borderline translucent. It was also the idyllic picture of middle class stability. The commercial 'main street' was always bustling with transactional activity, while the real estate market climbed with seemingly no ceiling in sight. The public schools, due to superior facilities, better paid and educated teachers, and a greater offering of extracurricular programs, were much better than the private schools, but the private schools survived because of religious devotion, as there was a church on every corner, but more so because of white fear: white fear of engagement with multicultural society, white fear of black people, white fear of children entering interracial relationships. White fear is the revenue generator for many industries in the United States, and as the world recently learned, it is also a powerful voter mobilization tool for historic political campaigns.

When I was in junior high school, the subdivision where my family lived began to slowly diversify. A Latino family moved into our cul-de-sac, which raised a few eyebrows, but the panic and paranoia really set in and cultivated convulsions as a town hobby, when the first black family bought a house down the block. Although I was young, I was old enough to understand the discussions that I could hear the neighbors having, and I was mature enough to find it disturbing. 'Here *they* come'... 'Once one comes, the rest will follow'... 'I heard there were blacks looking at the house on Manor...'

Of course, it was irrelevant that the family was a minister, a nurse, and their two children. They might as well have acted as co-leaders of the Crips. A crucial element of white fear is the fantasy of persecution. The black family is not simply looking to establish a good home in a safe neighborhood; they are foreign invaders, threatening to destroy property values and diminish community morale. The 'for sale' signs started appearing all around the neighborhood. When a single black man bought a house, followed by a childless black couple, the mass exodus only quickened. White flight happened throughout Lansing, and as more black families moved into town, many of them began to object to the public high school's mascot.

My alma mater's team name is the 'Rebels,' and their logo featured a Yosemite Sam lookalike in Confederate uniform carrying the secessionist flag. For reasons obvious to anyone not wearing the blinders of white rage and fear, black parents did not feel comfortable sending their children to a school proudly waving a flag that symbolizes their enslavement. White parents saw their glorification of a racist emblem not as worthy of reflection and correction, but as a sacred ritual to defend with self-centered fervor. Like maniacs, many whites began to stage marches around the school building, wearing confederate clothing and waving the flag. The small student population of African Americans suffered harassment from their white classmates. All the insanity escalated to such a tense level that Jesse Jackson announced a rally in Lansing. Before the civil rights leader arrived, the local government and the school board agreed to remove the flag from the school logo, and to eliminate it from all school sponsored displays.

I now live just east of Lansing in an Indiana town right over the border. One of my neighbors, also an alumnus of my high school, still references the rebel flag controversy as if it were some horrific assault on his life. '*They* made us take down our flag,' he will say, again referring to a dangerous and monolithic 'they' in an erasure of human identity, history, and complexity. For a short period of time, I worked as a substitute teacher at my old high school. It now has an almost entirely black student body. When I would answer the question, 'What do you do?' to a white local, inevitably I would receive a reaction of terror, as if my job was to fight prisoners in hand to hand combat – 'How do you do that?' … 'Wow, that must be rough.' My honest response – that I quite enjoyed it – would provoke shock and awe.

The south suburbs of Chicago aren't exactly Alabama territory under Bull Connor's authority, but in the 1990s, the white flight from the region happened so rapidly and dramatically that the *New York Times* reported on it with disbelief, and some researchers have concluded that suburbs near Lansing, such as Matteson and South Holland, saw the fastest white flight on record for the entire country.[4]

When Barack Obama became president elect in 2008, it seemed as if the entire country had transformed. The progressive orientation of young voters, of all races, and the diversification of American demographics, along with the unique charisma and brilliance of Obama, made what was unthinkable in my childhood an undeniable reality. Now, another previously unimaginable scenario has become all too real. A black family moved into the White House, and another form of white flight took off – white flight from political sanity, white flight from reality, and white flight from responsible citizenship.

The invisibility of Barack Obama created the unavoidability of Donald Trump. White Americans could not see Obama clearly. He was a threat. He was a symbol of their loss of authority. He was educationally, professionally, and, in terms of his family, superior to most of them, but they had to believe that he was inferior. Trump emerged as a white savior. When two thirds of Trump voters told pollsters that the 2016 election was America's 'last chance,' and when Trump promised that 'he alone' could repair the damage done to their beloved homeland, they and he were in transactional dialogue about the diversification of America, and his pledge to rescue the nation, returning it to white hands. The families of my neighborhood could not forcibly evict the black interlopers who destroyed the harmony of their community. They could only leave. Aggrieved white Americans are not going to leave the country, but they can change the aesthetic and authority of the country's institutions. Donald Trump issued the promise to do just that in overt language, while other Republican candidates have only occasionally offered a subtle nod to the racial anxiety of their base. Obama's fear that he 'came along twenty years too early' seems prescient. In reality, he came along too late. America should have elected a black president decades earlier, especially one with Obama's grace and intelligence, but his arrival, premature for the fragility of the white mind, produced the backlash of Trump's emergence.

It has little or nothing to do with economics. Studies demonstrated that Trump supporters, in the Republican primary, were actually wealthier than the constituencies for the Democratic candidates. *Five Thirty Eight* reported that the median household income among Trump supporters is $72,000 – not exactly hobo train jumpers.[5] If 'working class angst' explains the rise of Donald Trump, why is that working class black and Latino voters overwhelmingly supported Hillary Clinton?[6] If the 'white working class' feels 'forgotten and left behind,' why do they hate President Obama, who extended health care to twenty million Americans, doubled funding for Pell grants, advocated for free community college, fought to raise the minimum wage, and signed the Consumer Protection Financial Bureau into law, helping to protect low income home buyers from scam mortgages?

My wife and I would often shake our heads and curse the dark when we would ride through our neighboring town of Griffith, Indiana over the summer and fall of 2016. Trump signs in the yards of homes, and even in the windows of businesses, were ubiquitous eyesores. In the entire Northwest Indiana region, Griffith has become a major success story. New restaurants, shops, and breweries open on a monthly basis, and property values consistently increase. One of the major Chicago newspapers, along with Chicago's most popular business publication, has profiled Griffith, offering it as a model for small town economic vitality. Griffith, like Elkhart, Indiana, went from borderline bankruptcy to commercial triumph during the eight years of the Obama administration. In a lengthy profile of Elkhart, the *New York Times* revealed that when Obama took office in 2009, the unemployment rate was nearly twenty percent. Now, it is at three percent, but the town solidly supported Trump, even resorting to taunting the Latino members of a visiting high school basketball team with chants of 'Build the wall.'

Anything as unprecedented and unpredictable as Trump's victory is the result of several factors. Multiple causes coalesced to create the horror of Trump, but with the possible exception of sexism, none are more important than soft racism. The soft racist gets along with his black and Latino coworkers, waves to the Arab neighbors, and gives a friendly greeting to the parents of color at his child's school, but all the while, he feels that America is his country. The virtue of his whiteness gives him ownership. Should a black president, or a Black Lives Matter protest, or a Latino presence in his neighborhood threaten his sense of entitlement, superiority, and authority, he feels resentful, even hateful. Outwardly, the soft white racist treats people of color as if they are equal, but she actually believes that they are inferior – less worthy of liberty, opportunity, and protection under the law.

Most black and Latino Americans suspect as much, and they don't need a white millennial to tell them the news, but I would say that what I have heard from white neighbors, family members, and coworkers, confirms their worst suspicions. Now, the majority of white Americans have exposed their racism, no matter how soft, to the entire world, because a vote for Trump expresses, at a minimum, tolerance for bigotry, xenophobia, and misogyny. The best defense available to a Trump voter, among a wide range of pathetic options, is to claim that he or she voted for Trump, despite his disrespect of Hispanics, Muslims, the disabled, African Americans, and women. Tolerance translates to the cold message: 'Because your suffering and exclusion do not affect me, I'm going to vote for the guy who will cut my taxes, nominate anti-abortion Supreme Court justices, and isn't a woman who used a private email server.'

Many leftists won't acknowledge the totality of what Trump has exposed about America, because it is too ugly and painful. Well-intended, but misguided attempts at class solidarity with the forces of hatred will only enhance the present American nightmare. Like the influence of racism, another factor too obvious for many to believe is that hatred of women in power, and disrespect of women in general, fueled Trump's victory lap. To transition from the first black president to the first woman president was overload for the sensibilities of many Americans. In October, just over a month before the election, a tape emerged of Donald Trump bragging about groping women – 'grabbing them by the pussy,' to use his own words – without their consent. Within days, twelve women came forward to accuse Donald Trump of sexual assault and harassment. The tape and the allegations failed to significantly reduce Trump's support. The fact that Clinton's use of a private email server was a more controversial issue than Trump's brazen admission of sexual assault should send chills down the spine of American women when they consider their role in American culture. For many men and women of reason and logic, it is painful to contemplate how forty-two percent of women could vote for Trump – how the potential first woman president could lose more than four out of ten female votes to a man who demeans women by routine. To fail to specify what women supported Trump, however, does a disservice to the Americans who, more than any other demographical category, voted in bloc to stop him.

Ninety-four percent of black women voted for Hillary Clinton. Seventy-six percent of Latina women voted for Clinton. There was no competition among voters of color. Media commentators overrated Trump's performance with Hispanics, even though Clinton won seventy percent of their overall vote, but among African American and Hispanic women, the landslide was particularly steep. White women helped put Trump over the top, breaking for him fifty-three percent to forty-seven, with sixty-five percent of white women without a college degree voting for Trump.[7] White feminism has long faced accusations of ethnic provincialism from Angela Davis, Michele Wallace, and other feminist scholars of color. The Trump numbers reveal that a majority of white women identify first and foremost as white, consequences toward their own gender be damned.

The unapologetic nostalgia of Trump's 'Make America Great Again' campaign signifies a larger problem of white American delusion, of which racial anxiety and gender apprehension play only parts, albeit crucial ones. Resistance to multiculturalism and rage against the empowerment of women function as opposition to the future. No matter who occupies the Oval Office, the diversification of American demographics will not abate nor will the economic, social, and political developments of women's leadership. More women are graduating college than men. Their numbers in the professions, with the exception of engineering, are on the rise, while men are on the decline. Forty percent of American homes have 'female breadwinners,' and for the first time in American history, women can claim a majority of managerial positions.[8] Women are delaying marriage and childbearing, and while gender equality still does not exist, they enjoy roles of influence and authority unprecedented throughout American media, academic institutions, corporations, and local governments. Much of the Trump coalition – comprised primarily by white baby boomers and senior citizens – see these developments and pray for a return to the good, old days when blacks knew their place, Latinos were hard to find, Muslims were thousands of miles away, and women dutifully made dinner for their hardworking, Christian husbands.

One of the more amusing ironies of American life is the nostalgia for painful and stressful jobs that, when abundant, nearly everyone wanted to escape. Economic nostalgia coalesces with cultural regression in all of the maudlin pleas for a manufacturing renaissance in the Midwest. Despite the endless health risks, along with the emotional misery, of working in a textile mill or coalmine, the steady disappearance of manufacturing jobs, beginning in the 1970s, but somehow Barack Obama's fault, has produced tears of sadness and tears of rage. The tears are also for an illusion, and when Donald Trump promised, ad nauseam, to 'bring the jobs back,' he was acting as an illusionist on the level of David Copperfield.

Most Americans are intellectually unaware of the benefits of free trade, even though they experience them on a daily basis, but also suffer under the incorrect belief that globalization has caused an epidemic of unemployment, largely due to the death of American manufacturing. One of the widespread clichés Americans enjoy reciting is how 'we don't make anything here anymore.' The reality is that American manufacturing output is at an all time high. We make a lot of things here, but they aren't things you can buy at the convenience store or clothing shop. More important, they aren't things made by human beings. Automation and robotics have destroyed far more jobs than trade and globalization. Those jobs will not return, and if manufacturing makes a 'comeback' in the way that people hope, their disappointments and frustrations will intensify and multiply.

Bertram De Souza, the editorial writer for the *Vindicator*, in Youngstown, Ohio, one of the mid-size 'rust belt' cities hit hardest by the decline of steel employment in the United States, explains that for years Youngstown residents desperately prayed for a new steel mill to open nearby so that they might return to the past glory of full employment and prosperity when their city was one of the steel capitals of the world. A few years ago, it appeared as if they were about to receive manna from heaven. A French company opened a mill in Youngstown, investing $1.1 billion in the project. They hired 400 people. Robots and computers now make the product, and most of the workers earning high salaries, and collecting generous benefits, are engineers and computer scientists who sit in air conditioned offices all day, monitoring the machines.[9] Shortly after Donald Trump's election, he claimed a public relations victory when he used the promise of tax breaks and government contracts to bribe Carrier, an air conditioner manufacturer in Indiana, to reverse their plans to outsource 800 jobs to Mexico. American politicians and pundits debated the merits of Trump's unabashed exercise in crony capitalism. Many critics and economists warned that his maneuver would actually provide any intelligent CEO with an incentive to outsource jobs, given that the best-case scenario is bribery from the Trump administration. The debate is important, but as usual, most commentators missed the real story. The financial press reported a week after the Carrier announcement, that, in five to ten years, the company will automate the jobs that Trump 'saved.'[10] Such a twist brings to mind the observation that 'life is a tragedy to the man who feels, but a comedy to the man who thinks.'

Hillary Clinton was in a difficult position during the campaign. She could not correct Trump on trade, because Bernie Sanders, to her left during the primary, parroted the same anti-globalization nonsense as Trump, rattling up his supporters, who Clinton desperately needed to absorb. Meanwhile, Trump had colonized the right with his protectionist agenda. During the Republican primary, Ted Cruz stated the obvious when he rebutted Trump's pledge to impose tariffs and taxes on companies who manufacture overseas, with a warning to consumers that those same companies will make up for their losses by charging higher prices. 'They'll pass the tax onto you,' he said with little fanfare. The average television set cost $800 in 1964. Adjusted for inflation, that amounts to $5,800 in 2016. Because of free trade, and its reduction on prices of consumer goods, the typical TV now costs $500.[11] Simple economics, and the observable trends of the field, is not the equivalent of advanced physics, but the majority of American voters are uninformed on basic civics, let alone international economic theory and development. Rather than making political decisions according to an intellectual calculus, or even ideological bias, they run on the cheap fuel of emotion. The emotions often conflict, because they change issue to issue, so the American people are wildly inconsistent in their political beliefs and behavior. They are also hostile to the truth, because usually, the truth murders the merits of their emotional commitments.

For several years, one major American figure has spoken honestly and intelligently to the American people about manufacturing jobs and the inevitable transformations in employment trends throughout the country.

President Obama, with the aid of his Council of Economic Advisors, issued a lengthy report warning Congress to prepare legislation to deal with the inevitable job losses from automation.[12] He has also hosted White House events with experts from technological and business fields to discuss the incoming economic sea change. During a town hall meeting with voters, an Indiana resident asked Obama what he believes the United States government should do to 'bring the jobs back.' Obama gave a lengthy response, explaining the inalterable reality of automation by describing factories he has visited – factories that once employed ten thousand people, manufacture more product than ever before, but employ only hundreds of people. He then said, 'We have to make sure people are educated and trained for the jobs that are coming in now, because the jobs of the past are not coming back.' The Obama policy on manufacturing was to cooperate with local governments, universities, and small, mid-sized, and big businesses to create 'manufacturing hubs' to produce 'clean energy sources, 3-D printing, and nanotechnology,' and while manufacturing rose to its highest levels since the early 1990s during the Obama years, employment in that same sector stagnated. 'The days when if you are just willing to work hard,' Obama continued in his unsweetened analysis to his disgruntled voter, 'you can get a job at a plant for thirty or forty years are over, and they aren't going to be there for our kids.'[13]

For all of his vomitous bloviation about his worldly wisdom won in the boardrooms and on the construction sites of the real estate business, Donald Trump was the fantasy candidate and is the illusionist president. Barack Obama was the leader who dealt with the concrete. One of the problems to emerge in American culture is the abundance of abstractions – sentimental fixations impervious to factual penetration. Obama had little room for such abstractions, as he illustrated in his policies and rhetoric surrounding American manufacturing. Trump offers nothing more than sentimental abstraction – white authority in the face of irreversible diversification, nostalgia in reaction to unavoidable change, national pride in an increasingly global economy – and Trump's crucial constituencies loved him for it. It is debatable if even they believe him. Trump becomes a pro wrestler delivering a beating to a villainous opponent. The audience knows that it is a pre-scripted work, but screams and applauds anyway, because it feels good. Obama failed to offer feel good myths, and many voters turned on him. It is easier to stay in bed than face the uncertainty of a new day. In his explanation of complex developments, Obama is also a 'however' speaker. He will acknowledge that a problem is difficult to solve, but then transition to reason for hope. He will explain with nuance and subtlety the multiple facets of a particular issue. Donald Trump offers simple diagnoses and even simpler solutions.

Racial resentment, reactionary gender politics, and unrealistic hopes for time travel back to the 1970s job market coalesce to form a perfect picture of white, baby boomer anxiety. Baby boomers have exerted cultural control of America for decades, and due to mortality, they are now in the process of relinquishment. They do not intend to quietly hand over the keys to the pilot's cabin, as their endless sanctimony directed at 'snowflake' millennials demonstrates. Barack Obama, who is not a baby boomer, had a much more youth-oriented policy focus, and leadership style. He did not bow down to the boomer rites of passage and sensibilities. Donald Trump, a regression in many respects, is the ultimate defender of the boomer order. He behaves like a cliché out of *Mad Men* in his objectification of women, signals a return to white dominance of American culture, and promises to return all the hallmarks of boomer youth to the forefront of society. When asked about allegations of Russian hacking in the election he won, he said, 'I think computers have complicated lives very greatly. The whole age of the computer has made it where nobody knows what is going on.'

Donald Trump is president for Americans who are apprehensive about the personal computer. He will restore America to the paradise that existed before immigrants of color arrived, women applied for positions other than prone, and crazy machines made everything complicated. The Trump presidency presents a true threat and danger to civil liberties, human rights, and international peace, but for all of its severity, there is an element of silliness to it. It is that silliness that proves the futility of Trump, and empowers the legacy of Obama. The election of Trump was backlash to change that will not abate or end. The election of Obama, even in his absence from the White House, and while Republicans work to erase and sabotage his accomplishments, was the result and sign of change that will continue to develop. As odd and contradictory as it seems, the reality that elected Trump is the same reality that will protect Obama. If there is one truth of human history, however, it is contradiction, and in the words of Obama's old 'terrorist pal,' Bill Ayers – 'contradictions will save us.'

At the conclusion of *Invisible Man*, the unnamed narrator runs to escape a lynching party led by the black nationalist, Ras the Destroyer. Just when he thinks he has found safety and respite, a vicious group of white men surround him. They show no mercy in their hatred and hostility, attacking him with the violence of an angry mob. Then, to forever seal his status of invisibility, they trap him inside a coal filled manhole. By driving him underground, they hope that they will never have to lay eyes on him again. They cannot forget that he exists, and periodically, his presence might prod at the insecurities of their small minds, but if he is invisible, they can forget about him, enjoy their ignorance, and avoid confrontation with he who challenged their prejudice, and questioned their authority.

Donald Trump, the Republican Party with its ninety-three percent white membership, and the Trump coalition of overwhelmingly white voters are the political equivalent of the mob that attacked the invisible man. When they could not defeat Barack Obama at the polls, and they could not effectively undermine his legitimacy as president, they aspired to cast him underground and out of sight. Trump won with promises to entirely nullify the Obama agenda and legacy. He would sign the revocation of the Affordable Care Act, reverse regulations on Wall Street, undo Obama's executive orders, and preside over an American return to white, Christian cultural dominance with restrictions on immigration, surveillance of Muslims, and the assertion of unapologetic ethnic superiority. On November 8th, much of the world collectively cried and gasped at the unthinkable success of Trump. The surreal image of Donald Trump with his hand on the Bible, taking the oath of office, sent similar shockwaves of fear and outrage, even after several months for reality to sink in. He and his increasingly sycophantic Republican Congress have and will shred the social safety net, fire shots and missiles in the war on women, and make the world a more dangerous place – more likely to break out into war, and less able to deal with the consequences of climate change. White supremacists are empowered, claiming the Trump victory as their opportunity to invade the center of culture, and gain influence in politics, while civil rights organizations, immigrant advocacy groups, and Planned Parenthood are embattled, and struggle to prepare for several years of government-led campaigns to subvert and sabotage their work. And where is Obama?

His farewell address kept theme with his unbreakable optimism. He announced hope for the human spirit, and faith in the future of the American experiment in self-governance. He reminded his supporters that America has survived far worse crises, and that it has always managed to expand freedom, enlarge opportunity, and increase hospitality, even if it took great pain and suffering. He closed his speech with his greatest hit – 'Yes we can.' The speech was less poetic and more workmanlike than the typical Obama address. It was as if he was simply trying to offer a rudimentary reminder of American potential. If the people want to preserve their nation's potential, especially in the wake of such a stunning defeat, they must participate. What felt like a stirring anthem

chaos that threatens to undermine life. He carries with him, in the words of Ellison's unnamed narrator, 'the stench of death.' Appropriately, support for Donald Trump is dying – literally. His most reliable constituency is the white elderly, and his next most enthusiastic base of support is white baby boomers. The Obama constituency is living, and in the spirit of Theophrastus, who said, 'Where there is growth, there is life,' it is growing.

There are those who attack Obama for presiding over the demolition of the Democratic Party, and there are critics who claim that he is responsible for the rise of Donald Trump. Debates about his rhetorical style aside, there was never a moment in his presidency when he wavered from his commitment to elevate America's discourse, and provide an example of elegant citizenship and leadership. When historians, and confused ordinary Americans, seek to understand Barack Obama's contribution to American life and law (and why so few could see him clearly, how millions could elect an ignorant and manipulative vulgarian to succeed him, and how he could maintain such calm throughout all the turbulence) they could do no better than to read the closing thoughts of the invisible man:

> Being invisible and without substance, a disembodied voice, as it were, what else could I do? What else but to try to tell you what was really happening when your eyes were looking through?

★

On January 31st, 2017, President Donald Trump issued an executive order banning immigration from seven predominantly Muslim countries, ending entry of refugees from war-torn Syria, and enforcing a travel ban against visitation of the countries within the ban (Syria, Libya, Yemen, Somalia, Iran, Iraq, and Sudan). The order originally applied to immigrants who had already received green cards, and approval for admission from the Obama administration. It also restricted the reentry of people with dual citizenship who had the unfortunate timing of visiting one of the banned nations after Trump colored his jagged signature on official government paper. A federal judge in New York, and later Seattle, undercut much of Trump's order, declaring it unconstitutional and in violation of United States immigration law. Trump reacted by questioning the legitimacy of the justices who rendered the decisions, along with the entire judicial branch. Two weeks into his presidency, and he had already betrayed American principles of hospitality toward immigrants, Geneva Convention policy toward refugees, and the separation of church and state. As if those offenses were not sufficient to alarm the entire world, Trump's hostility toward the judicial branch of the American government provoked concern that he might create a constitutional crisis.

It is a long tradition in American politics that a former president allow his successor a grace period before expressing criticism of his policies. The unwritten regulation of political behavior allows the nation to acclimate itself to new leadership, and enables the novice president to gracefully prepare for the daunting tasks that undoubtedly await him. Bill Clinton, for example, waited until President Bush declared war on Iraq to question Bush's foreign policy, while Bush remained silent throughout almost the entirety of Obama's two terms in office. President Obama said that he would honor the presidential tradition of self-censorship as long as Trump did not threaten 'core American values.' Thousands of Americans overwhelmed airports to protest Trump's reactionary policy, just as the day after Trump's inauguration, millions of people around the world marched in cities, large and small, to oppose Trump's policies and rhetoric against women's liberty, autonomy, and equality. In the midst of an explosion of democratic energy, Barack Obama released an official statement through his spokesperson, a mere ten days after Trump's swearing in ceremony:

> President Obama is heartened by the level of engagement taking place in communities around the country. In his final official speech as president, he spoke about the important role of citizen and how all Americans have a responsibility to be guardians of our democracy – not just during an election, but every day. Citizens exercising their constitutional right to assemble, organize and have their voices heard by elected officials is exactly what we expect to see when American values are at stake. With regard to comparisons to President Obama's foreign policy decisions, as we've heard before, the president fundamentally disagrees with the notion of discriminating against individuals because of their faith or religion.[16]

There is not so much history as there is a continually developing present. The past and present collide along a continuum.

Tomorrow threatens to harm, just as much as it promises to heal. Barack Obama, as former president and private citizen, remains a player, decision maker, and leader in the unbroken struggle.

ACKNOWLEDGEMENTS

Many people provided important aid and assistance, directly and indirectly, to the creation of this book: First and foremost, Todd Swift – the founder and editorial director of Eyewear Publishing. His sharp and savvy vision of 'brief books for a busy world' with the Squint series demonstrates how publishing can remain powerful and indispensable with political analysis even in the cacophony of social media and 24 hour news cycles. Sarah Burk and Alexandra Payne, editors at Eyewear, gave this book a thorough reading, and offered insightful notes for improvement.

I would like to thank Bill Ayers and Jesse Jackson for their generosity of time and conversation. Their brilliance injected this book with crucial life, energy, and perspective. Alanna Ford, who manages to hold up the entire Rainbow/ PUSH structure on her shoulders, and look graceful while doing it, is a supporter, but more important, a friend I will forever love and cherish.

Douglas Swartz, a model of academic excellence in his capacity as English professor at Indiana University Northwest, provided valuable research assistance, without expectation of reward or compensation. He has my gratitude.

Last but not least, I would like to thank all of my family and friends, most especially my mother and father, whose encouragement and faith makes them coauthors on every book I have written and will write. John Keats wrote that 'beauty is truth.' Sarah, my amazing wife, is my beauty and truth. Thank you.

WORKS CITED

The Invisible Man

1. The Obama as 'vacationer-in-chief' narrative became pervasive, especially during his first term in office. For sample Fox News reports view https://www.youtube.com/watch?v=tbUTqeHiHDE or https://www.youtube.com/watch?v=KS8TBVHvdco. The *National Review* ran a characteristic polemic with the headline, 'Obama's Endless Vacation,' accessible here: http://www.nationalreview.com/article/386092/obamas-endless-vacation-matthew-continetti. Clarity on the issue is available at the Pulitzer Prize-winning project of the Annenberg Center at Penn State University, *Fact Check*: http://www.factcheck.org/2014/08/presidential-vacations/

2. The historical record of Gallup's polling on American attitudes associated with health care policy is available at http://www.gallup.com/poll/4708/healthcare-system.aspx.

3. The Health and Human Services report detailing how the Affordable Care Act enabled 20 million people to access health care is available at https://www.hhs.gov/about/news/2016/03/03/20-million-people-have-gained-health-insurance-coverage-because-affordable-care-act-new-estimates. *Fact Check* outlines how rising premiums are slower and lower due to ACA: http://www.factcheck.org/2015/02/slower-premium-growth-under-obama/. The *New York Times* reports drastic reductions in medical debt due to Obamacare: https://www.nytimes.com/2016/04/21/upshot/obamacare-seems-to-be-reducing-peoples-medical-debt.html?_r=0

4. The *Washington Post* studied what they call the 'new American malaise' in 2014: https://www.washingtonpost.com/news/the-fix/wp/2014/12/12/the-new-american-malaise/

5. In 2016, the *Washington Post* reported that two thirds of Trump voters interpreted his election as 'America's last chance,': https://www.washingtonpost.com/news/the-fix/wp/2016/12/02/two-thirds-of-trump-voters-viewed-the-election-as-americas-last-chance/?utm_term=.a78f6cf5754c

6. Pew Research Center has monitored demographic shifts throughout the United States: http://www.pewresearch.org/fact-tank/2015/04/08/reflecting-a-racial-shift-78-counties-turned-majority-minority-since-2000/

7. In 2016, the National Center for Education Statistics revealed that black women are the most educated group of Americans: http://www.pewresearch.org/fact-tank/2015/04/08/reflecting-a-racial-shift-78-counties-turned-majority-minority-since-2000/. The *Houston Chronicle* summarizes the Census report showing that Nigerian immigrants are the most educated Americans: http://www.chron.com/news/article/Data-show-Nigerians-the-most-educated-in-the-U-S-1600808.php#src=fb

8. Hedges' typically melodramatic and morose comments are audible and readable at *Democracy Now!*: https://www.democracynow.org/2010/12/20/chris_hedges_obama_is_a_poster

9. Filmmaker Steve McQueen offered his praise for Obama's cultural empowerment of black artists at the Whitney Museum of Art on May 1st, 2016, while in dialogue with public intellectual, Cornel West. A video of the entire discussion is available at https://vimeo.com/166363284.

10. *Newsweek* ran an excellent, albeit alarming, report in 2011, 'How Ignorant Are Americans?'. It is online at http://www.newsweek.com/how-ignorant-are-americans-66053.

11. Details on the bizarre and reactionary view of diversity among most Trump voters is available at https://www.washingtonpost.com/news/the-fix/wp/2016/12/02/two-thirds-of-trump-voters-viewed-the-election-as-americas-last-chance/

12. The insanity of Republican voters on the birther conspiracy theory is well documented. Read the *Politico* report, '51 Percent of GOP Voters: Obama Foreign' - http://www.politico.com/story/2011/02/51-of-gop-voters-obama-foreign-049554. *Business Insider*, among many other publications, reported that over six out of ten Trump supporters during the Republican primary believed that Obama was born in Africa: http://www.businessinsider.com/donald-trump-supporters-obama-muslim-fox-news-2015-9. Bill Moyers, veteran journalist and former official in the Johnson administration, produced and hosted an excellent Internet video broadcast in discussion with historians on how Donald Trump 'rode the big lie of birtherism to power.' It is available here: http://billmoyers.com/story/lest-we-forget/

13. In 2011, Donald Trump told Meredith Vieira, a reporter for the *Today* show, that his team of investigators were preparing to blow open the Obama birth scam. The video is on YouTube: https://www.youtube.com/watch?v=Blckpwk1voQ

14. In 2013, Gallup reported that the Republican Party is eighty-nine percent white: http://www.gallup.com/poll/160373/democrats-racially-diverse-republicans-mostly-white.aspx. Given that Trump won the presidency with less than ten percent of the black vote, and under twenty percent of the Latino vote, it is unlikely that the racial and ethnic makeup of America's two major parties have since changed.

15. Charles Blow, columnist for the *New York Times*, wrote about Sanders' dismissal of the Deep South, and the potential racial consequences: https://www.nytimes.com/2016/04/18/opinion/sanders-dismissesthe-deep-south.html.

16. *Medical Daily* offers insight into the high rate of anti-depressant use in the United States: http://www.medicaldaily.com/antidepressants-arent-taken-depressed-majority-users-have-no-disorder-327940

17. The *Atlantic* ran a report, with assiduous documentation, asserting that 2015 was the 'best year in history for the average human being': http://www.theatlantic.com/international/archive/2015/12/good-news-in-2015/421200/

A Man of Substance, Flesh, and Bone

1. During the presidential campaign of 2016, the *New Yorker* ran a profile of Trump's former ghostwriter, Tony Schwartz, who gave a disturbing account of his time with Trump: http://www.newyorker.com/magazine/2016/07/25/donald-trumps-ghostwriter-tells-all

2. The *Huffington Post* reports on Matthews' poor choice of words to describe the excitement of witnessing Obama's oratory: http://www.huffingtonpost.com/2008/02/13/chris-matthews-i-felt-thi_n_86449.html

3. The Academy Award winning film, *Nixon*, was written by Oliver Stone, Christopher Wilkinson, and Stephen J. Rivele. Oliver Stone also directed it. *Nixon* made its cinematic debut in 1995, and remains available on DVD and most streaming services.

4. Jesse Jackson provided his analysis of Obama's election during an interview I conducted with him in 2015.

These United States

1. Horace White and Elinor Langer provide a good summary of America's imperial intervention in Hawaii for the *Nation*: https://www.thenation.com/article/american-imperialism-when-it-all-began/

2. The *New York Times* obituary for Suharto gives ghastly detail to his history of human rights violations and violent censorship of dissent: http://www.nytimes.com/2008/01/28/

world/asia/28suharto.html. For original publication in *Mother Jones*, Noam Chomsky explained how US support was essential to the survival of Suharto's regime: https://chomsky.info/19990826/

3. The website of statistical wizard, Nate Silver, documents how white Americans who live in small towns comprise a mere twenty percent of the nation's population: https://fivethirtyeight.com/features/only-20-percent-of-voters-are-real-americans/

The South Side

1. The psychological literature on parental abandonment, and its consequences for the child, is vast, but an accessible treatment of the subject is available from *Psychology Today* at https://www.psychologytoday.com/blog/the-many-faces-addiction/201006/understanding-the-pain-abandonment

2. Cornel West made his remarks about cultural blackness on the *Tavis Smiley* program. The transcript of their discussion is available at http://www.pbs.org/wnet/tavissmiley/interviews/princeton-professor-dr-cornel-west-2/

3. Information about My Brother's Keeper, along with the transcript of Barack Obama's speech, is available at https://obamawhitehouse.archives.gov/my-brothers-keeper

4. The 2016 film, *Southside with You*, was written and directed by Richard Tanne. It is available on DVD and most streaming services.

5. The alarming details regarding childhood obesity in the United States are available from the Center for Disease Control: https://www.cdc.gov/healthyschools/obesity/facts.htm. *Politico* gives an inside account on the legislative and cultural fight surrounding Michelle Obama's attempt to get public schools to provide healthy lunches for children: http://www.politico.com/agenda/story/2016/03/michelle-obama-healthy-eating-school-lunch-food-policy-000066

6. President Obama's emotional statement on the massacre of children at Sandy Hook Elementary School in Newtown, Connecticut is viewable at https://www.youtube.com/watch?v=mIA0W69U2_Y

The Monster

1. For an excellent description and examination of 'The Paranoid Style in American Politics,' see the essay of the same name by historian Richard Hofstadter, in the November 1964 issue of *Harper's*: http://harpers.org/archive/1964/11/the-paranoid-style-in-american-politics/

2. The derangement surrounding the Clinton family is well-established and recorded, but for excellent sources see Hanna Rosin's essay, 'Among The Clinton Haters,' in the *Atlantic*: http://www.theatlantic.com/magazine/archive/2015/03/among-the-hillary-haters/384976/, or watch the documentary, *The Hunting of The President*, directed by Nickolas Perry and Harry Thomason.

3. For Chomsky's diagnosis and analysis of 'white fear of revenge,' read George Yancy's interview with him in the *New York Times* (March 18, 2015): https://opinionator.blogs.nytimes.com/2015/03/18/noam-chomsky-on-the-roots-of-american-racism/

4. Essayist and memoirist Ta-Nehisi Coates provides examples of white paranoia surrounding Obama in his essay for the *Atlantic*, 'How Breitbart Conquered the Media': http://www.theatlantic.com/politics/archive/2016/09/they-are-all-breitbart-now/499511/

5. Polling data on suspicion that Obama is a Muslim was reported in the *Hill*: http://thehill.com/blogs/blog-briefing-room/news/253515-poll-43-percent-of-republicans-believe-obama-is-a-muslim

6. The *Guardian* reported on the relatively widespread belief in American society that Barack Obama is the antichrist: https://www.theguardian.com/world/2013/apr/02/americans-obama-anti-christ-conspiracy-theories

7. Bill Ayers' recollections of his demonization and weaponization against Obama, along with his analysis of racial politics in the United States, come from an interview I conducted with him in 2016.

8. *New York* magazine summarized O'Reilly's racial anxiety in an appropriately headlined story, 'Fox News Slowly Loses Its Mind Over Election Results': http://nymag.com/daily/intelligencer/2012/11/fox-news-karl-rove-lose-mind-over-election-results.html

9. The *Washington Post* reported on Obama's 'boost' to the gun industry in 2015: https://www.washingtonpost.com/news/the-fix/wp/2015/03/11/barack-obama-may-have-been-at-least-a-9-billion-boon-to-the-gun-industry-so-far/?utm_term=.d298c0c2c237

10. The Southern Poverty Law Center documented the rise of state militias and hate groups during Obama's presidency: https://www.splcenter.org/news/2016/01/04/antigovernment-militia-groups-grew-more-one-third-last-year

11. *Politico* reported on Glenn Beck's assertion that Barack Obama hates white culture: http://www.politico.com/blogs/michaelcalderone/0709/Foxs_Beck_Obama_is_a_racist.html. The *Week* ran a lengthy examination of the belief among high ranking Republican officials and popular pundits that Obama is the most divisive president in history: http://theweek.com/articles/599246/republicans-say-obama-been-historically-divisive-thats-revealing

12. Jackie Calmes reported on Elkhart, Indiana for the *New York Times* in April of 2016: https://www.nytimes.com/2016/04/03/us/politics/obama-donald-trump-economy-indiana.html

13. Andrew Ross Sorkin interviewed Barack Obama for his assiduous report on the economic policy and legacy of Obama for the *New York Times Magazine* in May of 2016: https://www.nytimes.com/2016/05/01/magazine/president-obama-weighs-his-economic-legacy.html

14. The *Wall Street Journal* in a June 2016 report, 'Not Just the One Percent: The Upper Middle Class is Larger and Richer Than Ever,' detailed the income categories of the United States: http://blogs.wsj.com/economics/2016/06/21/not-just-the-1-the-upper-middle-class-is-larger-and-richer-than-ever/

15. Matt Phillips, for *Quartz*, provides a great summary of the workforce participation rate decline: https://qz.com/286213/the-chart-obama-haters-love-most-and-the-truth-behind-it/

16. *FiveThirtyEight* reported on the positive outcomes for the class of 2014: https://fivethirtyeight.com/datalab/the-class-of-2014-is-doing-pretty-well/

17. The *Fiscal Times* ran an informative report on the little discussed issue of medical errors and readmission: http://www.thefiscaltimes.com/2014/12/02/Drop-Hospital-Error-Rate-Saves-12B-2010

18. The *Consumer Reports* story ran in November of 2013: http://www.consumerreports.org/cro/news/2013/11/health-insurance-before-obamacare/index.htm

19. Bruce Bartlett wrote his essay for the *American Conservative* in October of 2014: http://www.theamericanconservative.com/articles/obama-is-a-republican/

The Messiah

1. Cornel West made his absurd remarks on *Democracy Now!* in November of 2012: https://www.democracynow.org/2012/11/9/tavis_smiley_cornel_west_on_the

2. The joint NYU and Stanford report on the human rights abuses of Obama's drone warfare campaign, 'Living Under Drones,' is available in its entirety at http://www.law.nyu.edu/news/global_justice_clinic_drones_report

3. Stephen Holmes reviewed Mark Mazzetti's investigation into Obama's drone warfare campaign for the *London Review of Books* in 2013: https://www.lrb.co.uk/v35/n14/stephen-holmes/whats-in-it-for-obama

4. The nonprofit, nonpartisan organization, National Priorities Project, keeps close record of American military spending, and its detraction of funds from more socially beneficial programs: https://www.nationalpriorities.org/. In September of 2015, the *Nation* ran an excellent, and disconcerting, report on the number of American military bases around the world: https://www.thenation.com/article/the-united-states-probably-has-more-foreign-military-bases-than-any-other-people-nation-or-empire-in-history/

5. The *Atlantic* story on the deleted slide, which implicated BP as negligent, and therefore, directly responsible for the spill is available at https://www.thenation.com/article/the-united-states-probably-has-more-foreign-military-bases-than-any-other-people-nation-or-empire-in-history/

6. *Rolling Stone* ran a useful summary of Obama's 'War on Pot,' under the same in 2012: http://www.rollingstone.com/politics/news/obamas-war-on-pot-20120216

7. Joni Lakin, a research professor for the Department of Education at Auburn University, has researched the harmful influence of Obama's K-12 education policy. Read a summary of her conclusions at Auburn's website: http://www.education.auburn.edu/news/coe-professor-joni-lakin-researches-dangers-high-stakes-school-testing/

8. *Stanford News* summarized Rice's views on education in 2013: http://news.stanford.edu/news/2013/april/rice-declining-schools-040513.html

9. In September of 2016, the *Chronicle of Higher Education* devoted an entire issue to study and scrutiny of Obama's policies on higher education, the contents of which are available at http://www.chronicle.com/specialreport/The-Obama-Issue/56

10. In 2013, The University of Chicago released a report, 'The Public Mood: White Malaise, but Optimism among Blacks and Hispanics': http://www.apnorc.org/projects/Pages/the-public-mood-white-malaise-but-optimism-among-blacks-hispanics.aspx

A President Without a Country

1. *Politico* offered a summary of Obama's 'Mister Hope' town hall: http://www.politico.com/story/2016/07/obama-race-critics-town-hall-225582

2. *Reason*, a libertarian magazine, ran a good report on Obama's statement about reduction in violence throughout the world, the criticism it provoked, and the accuracy of Obama's analysis: http://reason.com/blog/2016/07/24/obama-astonishes-sean-hannity-by-noting

3. *Politico* reported on Obama's decision to keep his schedule in Cuba after a terrorist attack in Brussels: http://www.politico.com/story/2016/03/barack-obama-cuba-baseball-game-brussels-attacks-221107

4. Jeffrey Goldberg interviewed Barack Obama and wrote an insightful story on the 'Obama doctrine' in foreign policy for the *Atlantic*: http://www.theatlantic.com/magazine/archive/2016/04/the-obama-doctrine/471525/

5. *US News and World Report* published a story on the 2015 World Happiness Report: http://www.usnews.com/news/articles/2015/04/24/world-happiness-report-ranks-worlds-happiest-countries-of-2015

6. On April 22, 2016, the *New York Times* ran a story with the sad headline, 'US Suicide Rate Surges to a 30 Year High': https://www.nytimes.com/2016/04/22/health/us-suicide-rate-surges-to-a-30-year-high.html. In 2011, *Live Science* reported on the decline of friendship in the United States: http://www.livescience.com/16879-close-friends-decrease-today.html

7. In 2014, Gallup reported on the staggering amount of Americans who feel disconnected from their work: http://

www.gallup.com/poll/181289/majority-employees-not-engaged-despite-gains-2014.aspx

8. Jackson made his remarks about Charleston's history on *Democracy Now!*: https://www.democracynow.org/2015/6/26/rev_jesse_jackson_take_down_the

9. In January of 2017, National Public Radio offered the transcript of Obama's final press conference as president: http://www.npr.org/2017/01/18/510291356/obamas-final-press-conference-as-president-annotated

From Obama to Trump: An Examination of American Psychosis

1. Obama addressed the bizarre and incoherent allegation that he was at fault for Trump's rise during a press conference. Reuters reported on his answer: http://www.reuters.com/article/us-usa-election-obama-idUSMTZSAPEC3AUCQoNA

2. Daniel Griswold, co-director of a program on American economics at George Mason University, wrote about the Ball State study for the *Los Angeles Times*: http://www.latimes.com/opinion/op-ed/la-oe-griswold-globalization-and-trade-help-manufacturing-20160801-snap-story.html

3. The *Washington Post* reported on the plethora of polls demonstrating that voters preferred Hillary Clinton on the economy: https://www.washingtonpost.com/news/the-fix/wp/2016/12/02/in-nearly-every-swing-state-voters-preferred-hillary-clinton-on-the-economy/

4. The *New York Times* reported on white flight in the south suburbs of Chicago in 1996: http://www.nytimes.com/1996/03/11/us/town-tries-to-keep-its-balance-in-wake-of-white-flight.html. Danielle Gordon wrote an excellent report on 'white flight taking off in the suburbs' for the December 1997 issue of the *Chicago Reporter*. Unfortunately, the story is no longer available online.

5. *FiveThirtyEight* studied the numbers on Trump's primary support, and broke the 'mythology of his working class support': https://fivethirtyeight.com/features/the-mythology-of-trumps-working-class-support/

6. Pew broke down the demographics that voted for Clinton and Trump, respectively: http://www.pewresearch.org/fact-tank/2016/11/09/behind-trumps-victory-divisions-by-race-gender-education/

7. *Quartz* ran a report, appropriately headlined, 'American Women Voted Overwhelmingly for Clinton, Except the White Ones': https://qz.com/833003/election-2016-all-women-voted-overwhelmingly-for-clinton-except-the-white-ones/

8. In 2014, Pew reported on the college graduation gap separating women from men: http://www.pewresearch.org/fact-tank/2014/03/06/womens-college-enrollment-gains-leave-men-behind/. In 2011, *Forbes* reported on the 'surprising job' that women are taking over: http://www.forbes.com/sites/jennagoudreau/2011/03/07/20-surprising-jobs-women-are-taking-over/#4d3094686f0b. The *New*

York Times reported on the rise of female breadwinners: http://www.nytimes.com/2013/05/30/business/economy/women-as-family-breadwinner-on-the-rise-study-says.html. According to a story in *Fusion*, women now barely edge out men in managerial positions: http://fusion.net/story/115596/women-now-hold-a-majority-of-all-management-and-professional-positions-in-the-u-s/

9. In 2016, National Public Radio spoke with Bertram De Souza about automation in Youngstown, Ohio: http://www.npr.org/2016/11/04/500728914/in-youngstown-ohio-support-for-trump-echoes-memories-of-local-political-hero

10. The CEO of United Tech, Carrier's parent company, was brazen in his admission that the Trump deal will only lead to further automation, and human job losses, as *Business Insider* reported: http://www.businessinsider.com/united-tech-ceo-says-trump-deal-will-lead-to-more-automation-fewer-jobs-2016-12

11. The Foundation for Economic Education, in 2016, explained the myriad benefits to American consumers of free trade: https://fee.org/articles/global-trade-is-why-your-television-did-not-cost-6-200-like-it-did-in-1964/

12. The Obama Administration Council of Economic Advisors report on automation is available at https://obamawhitehouse.archives.gov/blog/2016/12/20/artificial-intelligence-automation-and-economy

13. PBS provides the footage of Obama's remarks on 'bring the jobs back' during a town hall: https://www.youtube.com/watch?v=CKpso3vhZtw

14. In January of 2017, the *New York Times* ran a moving story on Obama's Chicago neighborhood connections, which featured comments from his former barber: https://www.nytimes.com/2017/01/09/us/politics/chicago-south-side-obama-farewell.html

15. *Bloomberg* reported on what the 2016 election 'taught us' about millennial voters: https://www.bloomberg.com/news/articles/2016-11-09/what-this-election-taught-us-about-millennial-voters

16. National Public Radio reported on Obama's opposition to Trump's immigration policy: http://www.npr.org/2017/01/30/512487565/obama-criticizes-trumps-immigration-ban-heartened-by-protests

BIBLIOGRAPHY

The following books are those that I either directly reference in the main text, or consider of such influence on my thoughts related to matters of race and politics, that they are worthy of my acknowledgement and gratitude.

Anderson, Carol. *White Rage: The Unspoken Truth of Our Racial Divide*. Bloomsbury Publishing: New York, 2016.

Aristotle. *Politics*. Stalley, R.F. (editor), Barker, Ernest (translator). Oxford University Press: Oxford, UK, 2009.

Ayers, Bill. *Public Enemy: Confessions of an American Dissident*. Beacon Press: Boston, 2013.

Barber, James David. *The Presidential Character: Predicting Performance in the White House*. Prentice-Hall: Upper Saddle River, NJ, 1972.

Burt, John. *Lincoln's Tragic Pragmatism: Lincoln, Douglas, and Moral Conflict*. Harvard University Press: Cambridge, MA, 2013.

Chait, Jonathan. *Audacity: How Barack Obama Defied His Critics and Created a Legacy that will Prevail*. Harper Collins: New York, 2017.

Chomsky, Noam. *Language and Politics*. Otero, C.P. (editor). AK Press: Oakland, CA, 2004.

Didion, Joan. *Political Fictions*. Alfred A. Knopf: New York, 2001.

Dionne, E.J. (editor), Reid, Joy-Ann (editor). *We are the Change We Seek: The Speeches of Barack Obama*. Bloomsbury Publishers: New York, 2017.

Dyson, Michael Eric. *The Black Presidency: Barack Obama and The Politics of Race in America*. Houghton Mifflin Harcourt: Boston, 2016.

Dyson, Michael Eric. *The Michael Eric Dyson Reader*. Civitas Books: New York, 2004.

Ellison, Ralph. *Invisible Man*. Modern Library: New York, 1952.

Ellison, Ralph. *The Collected Essays of Ralph Ellison*. Callahan, John F. (editor). Modern Library: New York, 1995.

Frady, Marshall. *Jesse: The Life and Pilgrimage of Jesse Jackson*. Simon and Schuster: New York, 1996.

Frey, William H. *Diversity Explosion: How New Racial Demographics are Remaking America*. Brookings Institution: Washington D.C., 2014.

Glassner, Barry. *The Culture of Fear: Why Americans are Afraid of the Wrong Things*. Basic Books: New York, 2000.

Harris-Perry, Melissa. *Sister Citizen: Shame, Stereotypes, and*

Black Women in America. Yale University Press: New Haven, 2011.

Hofstadter, Richard. *Anti-Intellectualism in American Life*. Alfred A. Knopf: New York, 1963.

King, Martin Luther. *I Have a Dream: Writings and Speeches That Changed The World*. Washington, James M. (editor). Harper Collins: New York, 1992.

King, Martin Luther. *Where Do We Go From Here: Chaos or Community*. Beacon Press: Boston, 1967.

Lasch, Christopher. *Haven in a Heartless World: The Family Besieged*. Basic Books: New York, 1977.

Mailer, Norman. *Mind of an Outlaw: Selected Essays*. Sipiora, Phillip (editor). Random House: New York, 2014.

Morrison, Toni. *Playing in the Dark: Whiteness and The Literary Imagination*. Harvard University Press: Cambridge, MA, 1992.

Obama, Barack. *Dreams from my Father: A Story of Race and Inheritance*. Three Rivers Press: New York, 1995.

Obama, Barack. *The Audacity of Hope: Thoughts on Reclaiming the American Dream*. Three Rivers Press: New York, 2006.

Painter, Nell Irvin. *The History of White People*. W.W. Norton: New York, 2010.

Plath, Sylvia. *The Collected Poems*. Hughes, Ted (editor). Harper and Row Publishers: New York, 1981.

Radkine, Claudia. *Citizen: An American Lyric*. Graywolf Press: Minneapolis, Minnesota, 2014.

Reeves, Richard. *President Kennedy: Profile of Power*. Simon and Schuster: New York, 1993.

Remnick, David. *The Bridge: The Life and Rise of Barack Obama*. Alfred A. Knopf: New York, 2010.

Sandburg, Carl. *The Complete Poems of Carl Sandburg*. Houghton Mifflin Harcourt: Boston, 2003.

Steele, Shelby. *A Bound Man: Why We Are Excited About Obama and Why He Can't Win*. Free Press: New York, 2008.

Traister, Rebecca. *All The Single Ladies: Unmarried Women and the Rise of an Independent Nation*. Simon and Schuster: New York, 2016.

Vidal, Gore. *Imperial America: Reflections on the United States of Amnesia*. Nation Books: New York, 2004.

Vidal, Gore. *The Last Empire: Essays 1992-2000*. Doubleday: New York, 2001.

Vidal, Gore. *United States: Essays 1952-1992*. Broadway Books: New York. 1993.

Wallace, Michele. *Invisibility Blues*. Verso: London, 1990.

Whitman, Walt. *Leaves of Grass* (The First Edition). Penguin: New York, 1855 (Reprint, 1981).

Whitman, Walt. *Democratic Vistas*. Folsom, Ed (editor). University of Iowa Press: Iowa City, 1871 (Reprint, 2009).

Younge, Gary. *The Speech: The Story Behind Dr. Martin Luther King Jr.'s Dream*. Haymarket Books: Chicago, 2013.